The Global Emergence of Constitutional Environmental Rights

Over the past 40 years, countries throughout the world have similarly adopted human rights related to environmental governance and protection in national constitutions. Interestingly, these countries vary widely in terms of geography, politics, history, resources, and wealth. This raises the question: why do some countries have constitutional environmental rights while others do not? Bringing together theory from law, political science, and sociology, a global statistical analysis, and a comparative study of constitutional design in South Asia, Gellers presents a comprehensive response to this important question. Moving beyond normative debates and anecdotal developments in case law, as well as efforts to describe and categorize such rights around the world, this book provides a systematic analysis of the expansion of environmental rights using social science methods and theory. The resulting theoretical framework and empirical evidence offer new insights into how domestic and international factors interact during the constitution drafting process to produce new law that is both locally relevant and globally resonant. Scholars, practitioners, and students of law, political science, and sociology interested in understanding how institutions cope with complex problems like environmental degradation and human rights violations will find this book to be essential reading.

Joshua C. Gellers is an Assistant Professor of Political Science at the University of North Florida and Fulbright Scholar to Sri Lanka. His work focuses on environmental rights and sustainable development. His articles have appeared in *International Environmental Agreements*, *Journal of Human Rights and the Environment*, and *Transnational Environmental Law*.

Law, Justice and Ecology

Series editor: Anna Grear, Cardiff Law School, Cardiff University, UK

In an age of climate change, scarcity of resources and the deployment of new technologies that put into question the very idea of the 'natural', this book series offers a cross-disciplinary, novel engagement with the connections between law and ecology. The fundamental challenge taken up by the series concerns the pressing need to interrogate and to re-imagine prevailing conceptions of legal responsibility, legal community and legal subjectivity, by embracing the wider recognition that human existence is materially embedded in living systems and shared with multiple networks of non-humans.

Encouraging cross-disciplinary engagement and reflection upon relevant empirical, policy and theoretical issues, the series pursues a thoroughgoing, radical and timely exploration of the multiple relationships between law, justice and ecology.

Titles in the series:

Contributions to Law, Philosophy and Ecology
Exploring Re-Embodiments
Edited by Ruth Thomas-Pellicer, Vito De Lucia and Sian Sullivan

Law as if Earth Really Mattered
The Wild Law Judgment Project
Edited by Nicole Rogers and Michelle Maloney

Forging a Socio-Legal Approach to Environmental Harms
Global Perspectives
Edited by Tiffany Bergin and Emanuela Orlando

The Global Emergence of Constitutional Environmental Rights
Joshua C. Gellars

The Global Emergence of Constitutional Environmental Rights

Joshua C. Gellers

Routledge
Taylor & Francis Group
LONDON AND NEW YORK

First published 2017
by Routledge

2 Park Square, Milton Park, Abingdon, Oxfordshire OX14 4RN
711 Third Avenue, New York, NY 10017

Routledge is an imprint of the Taylor & Francis Group, an informa business

First issued in paperback 2018

British Library Cataloguing in Publication Data
A catalogue record for this book is available from the British Library

Library of Congress Cataloging in Publication Data
Names: Gellers, Joshua C., author.
Title: The global emergence of constitutional environmental rights / Joshua C. Gellers.
Description: New York, NY : Routledge, 2017. | Series: Law, justice and ecology | Includes bibliographical references and index.
Identifiers: LCCN 2017017990 | ISBN 978-1-138-69649-5 (hbk)
Subjects: LCSH: Environmental law | Constitutional law. | Environmental justice. | Environmental law, International.
Classification: LCC K3585 .G45 2017 | DDC 344.04/6—dc23
LC record available at https://lccn.loc.gov/2017017990

ISBN: 978-1-138-69649-5 (hbk)
ISBN: 978-0-367-02422-2 (pbk)

Typeset in Baskerville
by FiSH Books Ltd, Enfield

To my parents,
Paul and Gayle,
who gave me the world and the courage to improve it.

Contents

Figures and tables

Figures

Tables

Abbreviations

AISLS	American Institute for Sri Lankan Studies
AL	agricultural land
ASEAN	Association of Southeast Asian Nations
CEA	Central Environmental Authority
CL	civil liberties
DAC	Development Assistance Committee
EFL	Environmental Foundation Limited
EIA	environmental impact assessment
EIS	environmental impact statement
EM	ecological modernization
ENGO	environmental non-governmental organization
EPL	Environmental Protection License
ES	English School
FDI	foreign direct investment
FECOFUN	Federation of Community Forestry Users, Nepal
GDP	gross domestic product
GDPpc	gross domestic product per capita
GNI	gross national income
HRC	Human Rights Council
HRL	human rights legacy
IACHR	Inter-American Commission on Human Rights
ICCPR	International Covenant on Civil and Political Rights
ICDC	Interim Constitution Drafting Committee
ICESCR	International Covenant on Economic, Social and Cultural Rights
ICSI	international civil society influence
IGO	inter-governmental organization
ILO 169	International Labor Organization Convention Number 169
INGO	international non-governmental organization
IR	international relations
IRB	Institutional Review Board
IUCN-Nepal	International Union for Conservation of Nature, Nepal

LA	land area
LD	level of democracy
MDG	Millennium Development Goal
MI	monetary incentives
MNC	multinational corporation
NBA	net bilateral aid
NEA	National Environmental Act
NGO	non-governmental organization
NRD	natural resource dependency
NRPP	Natural Resource People's Parliament
NRR	total natural resource rents
OAS	Organization of American States
ODA	net official development assistance
PD	population density
POP	population
PR	political rights
PRC	Public Representations Committee
RC	regime characteristics
RD	regional diffusion
SAC	South Asian constitution
SIAS	Southasia Institute of Advanced Studies
TAN	transnational advocacy network
UDHR	Universal Declaration of Human Rights
UIA	Union of International Associations
UNECE	United Nations Economic Commission for Europe

Acknowledgments

This book presents a whole story that could not have been told without its constituent parts, some of which were previously published as articles. I am thankful to Cambridge University Press, Edward Elgar (www.e-elgar.com/), and John Wiley and Sons for allowing me to reproduce excerpts or revised versions of the following published works:

"Environmental Constitutionalism in South Asia: Analyzing the Experiences of Nepal and Sri Lanka." *Transnational Environmental Law* 4(2): 395–423 (2015);

"Explaining the Emergence of Constitutional Environmental Rights: A Global Quantitative Analysis." *Journal of Human Rights and the Environment* 6(1): 75–97 (2015);

"Greening Constitutions with Environmental Rights: Testing the Isomorphism Thesis." *Review of Policy Research* 29(4): 522–542 (2012).

I would not have been able to execute this ambitious project without the guidance and wisdom of my committee members at the University of California, Irvine (UCI): Richard Matthew, Wayne Sandholtz, Diana Kapiszewski, Joe DiMento, and David Feldman. Each of you brought a unique perspective that informed a research agenda that did not fit neatly into a single disciplinary box. Your lasting encouragement motivated me to squeeze a dissertation into a book.

Thanks to the Department of Political Science and the Center for Global Peace and Conflict Studies at UCI for funding my fieldwork in Nepal and Sri Lanka. I also owe a debt of gratitude to the School of Social Sciences for awarding me fellowships that allowed me to focus on my research. Finally, I wish to acknowledge the UCI Environment Institute, Center in Law, Society, and Culture, and the Center for Unconventional Security Affairs for their financial support.

My field research would not have been possible without the help of kind and generous colleagues in Nepal and Sri Lanka. Hari Dhungana, Kamal Devkota, Ira Unamboowe, and Camena Guneratne helped with logistical issues, lent institutional support, and provided assistance that proved essential during my short stints abroad. I offer my deepest appreciation to the Southasia Institute of Advanced Studies and Open University of Sri Lanka for granting me institutional affiliation while I was in Kathmandu and Colombo.

As I transitioned from graduate student to faculty member, I met some incredibly talented people in the small world of environmental rights scholarship. Jimmy May and Erin Daly inspired my interest in environmental rights while I was in graduate school and later afforded me the opportunity to serve as a Visiting Scholar-in-Residence in Global Environmental Constitutionalism at Delaware Law School during the spring of 2015. Christopher Jeffords has been a fantastic co-author and confidante. Louis Kotzé is an established scholar of environmental constitutionalism who has helped me realize my potential. Anna Grear, editor for the Law, Justice and Ecology series at Routledge, has been unwavering in her support for me and my research, and provided me with professional opportunities for which I will never be able to thank her enough. Ben Cashore invited me to speak at Yale while I was still a doctoral student and has since become a steadfast colleague. John Knox saw the merit in my Enviro Rights Map project and continues to do important work advancing environmental rights at the international level.

I would like to express my gratitude to the chairs, discussants, and attendees at conferences, workshops, and symposia at Yale University and Delaware Law School, whose research and helpful comments have in some way influenced the direction of this book. Evan Schofer gave me critical feedback about my treatment of world society theory. Tom Ginsburg helped found Constitute Project (www.constituteproject.org/), a dynamic resource for researching constitutions that made my work easier. Thanks also to Colin Perrin, my commissioning editor at Routledge, who was as helpful and responsive as anyone could hope an editor might be.

Finally, I would like to thank members of my small but fiercely united family. My parents, Paul and Gayle, sacrificed so I could have opportunities they did not. Their love is indefatigable. My aunt, Diane Spinell, has always provided avenues for my academic enrichment and was a terrific travel companion during my Nepal trip. My maternal uncle, Rick Spinell, encouraged me to keep on the path to earning the PhD when the distance seemed too great. My paternal uncle, the late Tuvia Ben-Shmuel Yosef, instilled within me a lasting passion for the study of law and a desire to help others obtain justice. Finally, Brett Daniel Gellers, an ardent defender of logic and reason who does not suffer fools gladly, has in some ways been the older brother I never had.

Chapter 1

Constitutions, the environment, and human rights

The heavy monsoon air assaulted my travel-worn body right as I stepped onto the tarmac at Tribhuvan International Airport in Kathmandu, Nepal. It was nearly 10 pm. I shuffled through customs half asleep, alert only enough to notice the modest size of the terminal, the anachronistic use of wood paneling, and my inability to tap into a wireless network on my cellphone. After collecting my checked luggage I headed outside, where a taxi hired by my hotel waited to receive me. The airport seemed an island of light amidst the sea of darkness filling the Nepalese night. A soft rain began to trickle down from the illimitable skies.

Once inside the cab, I felt my fatigue quickly dissolve as a flicker of curiosity ignited my attention. The taxi driver expertly navigated rough roads and tortuous alleyways with a kind of certainty that stood in stunning contrast to my complete sense of alienation. I knew where I was geographically speaking, but that knowledge failed to register any concrete meaning in my present state. I turned my gaze out the passenger window.

The only bits of country accessible to my visual field were those elements crudely illuminated by the yellow headlights of our car. As we zoomed along the dampened streets, panic crept its way up my throat until it formed a knot at the back of my mouth. The external world rendered cognizable only by the small golden spheres constantly being chased by the taxi elicited terror, then disbelief. Multi-story buildings gaped like the skeletal remains of faces blown out by indiscriminant aerial bombing campaigns. Trash and rubble commingled in random elevated patches along the roadways. Feral dogs in search of a late supper zipped up and down saturated heaps of garbage. Upon beholding these unexpected sights I was forced to recall why I had ventured nearly 8,000 miles to this unique country in the first place—because Nepal had recently added environmental rights to its national constitution. Clearly the gulf separating law and practice remained vast, but I didn't fly to this pivotal pocket of Asia in order to lambaste a developing country for its inability to implement environmental law. I was here to understand why a growing chorus of states echoed a preference for enacting constitutional environmental rights.

Introduction

Over the past four decades, countries throughout the world have adopted human rights pertaining to environmental protection and governance in their respective national constitutions. Such legal provisions are collectively known as "constitutional environmental rights." Interestingly, states with constitutional environmental rights appear to have little else in common; they vary widely in terms of their geographic location, history, human and natural resources, political system, size, and wealth. At the same time, environmental rights do not (yet) enjoy universal recognition among governing charters across the globe. This observation poses an empirical puzzle for social scientists—*Why do some countries have constitutional environmental rights while others do not?*

I argue that the phenomenon identified above has occurred as a result of international norms that *constrain* constitution drafting processes, compelling states to adopt human rights related to the natural environment, and *constitute* state identities, socializing countries to treat environmental protection as a proper domain of state authority and view environmental quality as fundamentally related to human rights. I also contend that the global emergence of constitutional environmental rights is not driven by individual state calculations regarding opportunities to enhance power or material wealth. The mixed-methods study contained within this book rigorously tests the validity of these two arguments.

But before proceeding to examine the reasons why environmental rights have increasingly found a home in national constitutions across the world, it helps to first understand why these rights are important and how this book contributes to existing knowledge on the subject. To begin, how are environmental rights distinct from other institutional mechanisms intended to address environmental problems? The worldwide spread of environmental rights represents an important development worthy of empirical examination for reasons related to morality, legitimacy, authority, and identity. First, by raising the prerogative of environmental protection to the level of importance afforded human rights, states assign universal *moral* significance to the task of safeguarding the environment. This formal reconceptualization of the human–environment relationship suggests that environmental rights are fundamental to the wellbeing of citizens, marking a significant shift in constitutional design and legal thinking. Second, constitutional environmental rights add new *legitimacy* and urgency to the cause of environmental protection. By linking the environment to human rights, environmentalists gain the clout of institutions and resources central to the international human rights movement (Nickel 1993, p.283), potentially resulting in a greater capacity to mobilize support for the resolution of environmental problems. Third, placing environmental rights within a constitution imbues them with the highest level of legal *authority* available in a society governed by the rule of law (Gravelle 1997, p.635). Incorporating environmental rights into constitutional frameworks avoids placing the onus for environmental protection solely on legislative bodies whose decisions may hinge on a narrow majority, and makes removal of such provisions politically cumbersome (Brandl & Bungert 1992, p.4). Finally, once these rights are formally adopted, they become woven into the fabric of a state's national *identity*. Constitutional entrenchment of environmental rights "results in the identification of environmental protection with expressions of national pride and character" (Brandl & Bungert 1992, pp.4–5).

To be sure, the adoption of constitutional environmental rights may produce lasting effects related to the project of environmental governance. Although in general constitutions have a relatively short shelf life (Elkins et al. 2009, p.1), previous iterations may serve as benchmarks for later versions, constraining the decisions of future drafters (Osiatynski 1994). In the near term, constitutional environmental rights may raise the bar for domestic environmental governance and amplify popular expectations about the state's capacity to safeguard the environment, making it difficult for political leaders to rescind such ambitions later. In short, the act of situating environmental rights within a constitution enhances their institutional "stickiness," leaving a legacy that may influence reform efforts in the future.

At the same time, one should remain cautious when speculating about the utility of constitutional rights in general. Laws on the books do not necessarily translate to laws in action. The very act of drafting a constitution carries such normative weight that "it is invoked by regimes that make no pretense of submitting to constitutional control" (Ginsburg 2003, p.9). Therefore, while evaluating the efficacy of constitutional environmental rights remains a work in progress (e.g., Boyd 2012; Gellers & Jeffords 2015; Jeffords 2016; Jeffords & Minkler 2016), it stands to reason that environmental rights represent important legal tools that may hold significant promise for addressing issues occupying the nexus between human rights and the environment.

So how does this book augment the current understanding about constitutional environmental rights? This text complements the impressive body of mainly descriptive scholarship on constitutional environmental rights through its application of social science methods to empirical inquiries and its explication of an interdisciplinary approach to explaining the emergence of these provisions. In particular, it presents the first global statistical analysis that systematically tests different theories that may explain why countries adopt constitutional environmental rights. Drawing on political science, sociology, and law, it also provides the first theoretical framework designed to sketch out the mechanisms through which constitutional environmental rights have expanded throughout the international system. In addition, this study offers the first social scientific account of the development of constitutional environmental rights in Nepal and Sri Lanka, contributing a rare comparative study to the "relatively unexplored area" (Khilnani et al. 2013, p.2) of South Asian constitutions (SACs).

The remainder of this introductory chapter proceeds as follows. First, I define environmental rights. Second, I discuss the three forms in which environmental rights appear in legal institutions. Third, I trace the history of environmental rights as they developed through human rights institutions at the international level. Fourth, I examine regional developments associated with environmental rights. Fifth, I describe the development of constitutional environmental rights at the national level. Sixth, I review two of the main controversies surrounding constitutional environmental rights. Finally, I outline the structure and content of the remainder of the book.

Definitions and purpose

"Environmental rights" can be defined in different ways depending on the object or entity to which they apply. To whom are these rights to be bestowed? Environmental rights can be construed as rights held by the environment itself to protect against harm caused by an external force. Ecuador's 2008 constitution includes an entire chapter devoted to these so-called "rights of nature." In particular, Article 71 states: "Nature, or Pacha Mama, where life is reproduced and occurs, has the right to integral respect for its existence and for the maintenance and regeneration of its life cycles, structure, functions and evolutionary processes" (Ecuador Const., tit. II, ch. 7, art. 71 (2008)). However, environmental rights are more commonly understood to mean "the reformulation and expansion of existing human rights and duties in the context of environmental protection" (Shelton 1991, p.117). This definition characterizes such legal provisions as explicitly human centered. The question regarding whether environmental rights should include rights of the environment itself or refer exclusively to rights held by humans remains a subject of considerable debate (e.g., Taylor 1997; Bruckerhoff 2008). I return to this issue later in the chapter.

After identifying the intended referent of the environmental rights, it is important to understand the role of various state and non-state actors in securing these rights. Governments, either at the national or international level, as the main guarantors of rights, are said to possess negative or positive duties to the party being protected. For instance, "governments have negative duties to refrain from actions that generate large risks of damage to human life and health" while they "also have a duty to protect inhabitants of their territories against environmental risks generated by either governmental or private agencies" (Nickel 1993, p.286). In addition, depending on the version of the right articulated, individuals and organizations may similarly "have a duty to refrain from activities that generate unacceptable levels of environmental risk" and, in situations resulting in environmental harm, "a duty to restore the environment and compensate victims" (Nickel 1993, p.286). However, environmental rights signal more than responsibilities; they may also denote certain freedoms. For individuals or groups, environmental rights explicitly or implicitly entail a freedom *from* environmental damage while some specific environmental rights directly recognize a freedom *to* obtain justice for environmental wrongs committed. The particular phrasing used in the construction of environmental rights thus indicates who or what is to be protected, by whom, and to what end.

What purpose do environmental rights serve? First, environmental rights seek to unite and advance the protection of human rights and the environment through formal legal means. Neither objective can be fully attained through the pursuit of the other; protecting the environment does not necessarily lead to the fulfillment of human rights obligations, and safeguarding human rights may not produce positive environmental outcomes. Yet, in order to survive, humanity requires an environment conducive to its continued existence. One cannot enjoy the most fundamental human right, the right to life, if the environment in which one lives suffers degradation that seriously imperils human health (Atapattu 2002, p.69). In order to "protect human life, our environmental life support system must be maintained and protected" (Thorme 1991, p.301). Environmental rights thus provide tools through which the goals of safeguarding both human rights and the environment may be pursued simultaneously. Second, environmental rights offer legal mechanisms that enable individuals and groups to redress environmental grievances. In particular, this relatively new set of rights may help vulnerable populations achieve social justice. As "the worst victims of environmental harm tend also to be those with the least political clout" (Dommen 1998, p.3), environmental rights may bolster the ability of poor, marginalized groups to gain access to the legal system in order to pursue corrective, restorative, and compensatory outcomes that bring society closer to a just order. Some preliminary analyses suggest that procedural environmental rights, for example, may increase the likelihood of achieving environmental justice outcomes (Gellers & Jeffords 2015).

Forms of environmental rights

Environmental rights generally appear in one of three forms—procedural, substantive, or solidarity rights. Procedural environmental rights refer to legal provisions that "promote the transparency, participation, and accountability that form the cornerstones of environmental governance" (Bruch et al. 2001, p.135). Such rights guarantee "(1) freedom of association, (2) access to information, (3) public participation in decision-making, and (4) access to justice" in environmental matters (Bruch et al. 2001, p.176).[1] Procedural environmental rights can serve as a means of achieving objectives related to the environment or as an end unto themselves through the promotion of discourse and democracy (May 2013, p.28). According to Boyd (2012), 28 countries have constitutions that feature procedural environmental rights.[2] As an example, Albania's constitution guarantees citizens "the right to be informed about the status of the environment and its protection" (Albania Const., ch. IV, art. 56 (2012)). Observers have characterized these rights as among the most important recent developments in human rights law (Boyle 2012) and synonymous with the very concept of environmental rights (Atapattu 2002, p.72).

Substantive environmental rights refer to rights within the corpus of international human rights law that may apply when environmental problems animate human rights concerns. Relevant substantive rights that may intersect with environmental issues include "the right to life, the right to health, the right to an adequate standard of living, and the right to privacy" (Atapattu 2002, p.96).[3] For example, some writers argue that a good environment is necessary to enjoy the right to life, for "without the environment, no life is possible" (Rehbinder & Loperena 2001, p.283). Utilizing existing human rights to pursue the protection of environmental rights may prove more effective than relying on procedural environmental rights alone. As one scholar explains, "even if procedural or participatory rights are fully realized, and perfectly distributed throughout civil society, it is entirely possible that a participatory and accountable polity may opt for short-term influence rather than long-term environmental protection" (Anderson 1996, p.10). Increasing the opportunity for public debate and engagement does not necessarily mean pro-environmental outcomes will materialize.

Solidarity environmental rights establish a specific right relating to the environment that, unlike other forms of rights that states may ensure on their own, mandate global participation for successful enforcement. Solidarity rights are labeled as such because they speak to the idea that a broad community of actors and universal cooperation is required to "[attain] a livable world" (Hassan 1983, p.54). Solidarity rights draw intellectual inspiration from "the post-World War II anti-colonial revolutions that introduced the principles of self-determination and nondiscrimination" (McClymonds 1992, p.591). Other solidarity rights include the right to development and the right to peace. These rights are often considered "third generation" rights within the genealogy of international human rights (Marks 1981). Since 1976, Portugal's constitution has included a solidarity environmental right constructed using language common to these kinds of provisions: "Everyone shall possess the right to a healthy and ecologically balanced human living environment and the duty to defend it" (Portugal Const., tit. III, ch. II, art. 66(1) (1976)). While environmental rights have become prevalent across the globe in recent decades, experiences from within the United States suggest that some courts have difficulty "with the idea of conferring constitutional status on environmental rights" (Howard 1996, pp.405–406). Such rights have not been readily interpreted to possess the innate legal force commensurate with existing fundamental rights, and the ultimate viability of expressing environmental rights in solidarity form is a topic that has aroused considerable debate.[4] However, judicial receptivity to environmental rights at the state level within the U.S. has begun to shift as of late, as evidenced by the decision in the *Robinson Township*[5] case, in which the Pennsylvania Supreme Court declared unconstitutional parts of an oil and gas law that conflicted with the state's obligations under the Environmental Rights Amendment to its constitution (Dernbach et al. 2015).

International developments

In order to accurately describe the development of environmental rights at the international level, it is imperative to first discuss the trajectory of international human rights and how environmental rights evolved through the process of an ongoing global discourse on human rights.

International and regional human rights

While the historical roots of human rights can be traced back to ancient Greece and Rome with the concept of natural law, the modern understanding of human rights arrived on the international stage at the conclusion of World War II. The ascendance and ultimate demise of Nazi Germany forced international actors to confront issues of global morality and the proper role of the international community in protecting minorities and other vulnerable groups. The world came to recognize that the domestic laws and policies of nation-states could not escape judgment under the banner of moral relativism; some norms of behavior must apply universally to all members of international society. Following the conclusion of World War II, the international community coalesced around the idea that "[c]ertain actions are wrong, no matter what; human beings are entitled to simple respect at least" (Weston 1984, p.261).

Thus began the emergence of a global recognition of the need to protect human rights. Seizing upon this moment in history, states formed the United Nations, pledging to strive for "universal respect for, and observance of, human rights and fundamental freedoms for all without distinction as to race, sex, language, or religion" (UN Charter, ch. 1, art. 1, § 3 (1945)). In 1948, these ambitions became formally codified in the Universal Declaration of Human Rights (UDHR). With language clearly inspired by the atrocious acts committed during World War II, the UDHR stipulated that "it is essential … that human rights should be protected by the rule of law" (Universal Declaration of Human Rights). In addition, the UDHR included rights corresponding to what would later become known as the three generations of human rights (Marks 1981; Weston 1984, pp.264–267).

First generation rights appear in Articles 2–21 of the UDHR. This generation of rights consists of civil and political rights, such as the freedom of speech and the right to vote, which mandate government non-interference in citizen participation in governing activities. These rights owe an intellectual debt to the French and American revolutions, which sought to secure human rights through freedom from governmental intrusion. Second generation rights appear in Articles 22–27. These rights consist of economic and social rights, such as the right to a living wage and fair working conditions, which require active government involvement. This generation of rights came about as a result of "social upheavals … arising from abuses of the rights of the first generation" and found philosophical substantiation in "socialist and Marxist writings" (Marks 1981, p.438). The distinction between first and second generation rights is similar to the discussion of negative and positive duties in that first generation rights reflect a freedom from government influence, whereas second generation rights seek the enjoyment of certain freedoms that require government intervention (Nickel 1993). Finally, third generation rights are intimated in Article 28, which asserts that "everyone is entitled to a social and international order in which the rights set forth in this Declaration can be fully realized" (Universal Declaration of Human Rights). This last group of rights grew out of "major planetary concerns which, although they were always present and sometimes felt acutely in the past, have taken on a renewed urgency at a time when the legislative process in the field of human rights is particularly receptive" (Marks 1981, pp.440–441). Third generation rights are "unique in that the world community … owes a moral, and now a legal, duty to safeguard the continued existence of mankind and the quality of life, as a recognized rubric of international public policy" (Gormley 1990, p.105). Such rights differ from first and second generation rights in that they "may be both *invoked against* the State and *demanded* of it" (Vasak, as cited in Marks 1981, p.441). Third generation rights include the right to "environment, development, peace, the common heritage, communication, and humanitarian assistance" (McClymonds 1992, pp.591–592).

The first two generations of human rights gained additional explication in 1966, when the United Nations General Assembly approved both the International Covenant on Civil and Political Rights (ICCPR) and the International Covenant on Economic, Social and Cultural Rights (ICESCR).[6] The ICCPR addresses the need to protect first generation rights such as the right to life, the right to liberty and security of person, and the right to freedom of religion. In addition, the agreement calls for the protection of rights not included in the UDHR, such as the right of all peoples to self-determination, and establishes a Human Rights Committee composed of 18 elected experts charged with monitoring compliance. The ICESCR enumerates second generation rights such as the right to safe and healthy working conditions, the right to form trade unions, and the right to education. However, unlike the ICCPR, the ICESCR does not feature language advocating for immediate implementation of its provisions, urging instead that states actively pursue full protection of the rights contained within the treaty to the extent possible given the resources available.

During the time that international human rights began to gain global recognition, two regional human rights systems emerged in Europe and the Americas. Created upon agreement among members of the Council of Europe in 1950, the European Convention for the Protection of Human Rights and Fundamental Freedoms (European Convention) represents an early regional effort to provide for the protection of human rights. Based on a draft of the ICCPR, the European Convention stands as "the most advanced and successful international experiment in the field [of human rights]" (Weston 1984, p.277). The European Convention also produced two significant regional human rights institutions—the European Commission of Human Rights and the European Court of Human Rights.

Two years prior to the arrival of the European Convention, the Ninth Pan-American Conference adopted the American Declaration on the Rights and Duties of Man and established the Organization of American States (OAS). In 1959, provisions for the protection of human rights within the OAS system obtained institutional support with the creation of the Inter-American Commission on Human Rights (IACHR). A decade later, the American Convention on Human Rights (American Convention) was adopted at the Inter-American Specialized Conference on Human Rights, charging the IACHR with implementing the convention and establishing the Inter-American Court of Human Rights. The American Convention, likely influenced by European developments in the area of human rights, entered into force in 1978.

While none of these international or regional agreements deals explicitly with environmental rights, these innovations may have provided a legal backdrop for future consideration of issues at the intersection of human rights and environmental protection. In his seminal article on the subject, Sax (1990) argues that environmental rights may be extrapolated from both first generation (negative) and second generation (positive) rights. First generation rights such as those guaranteeing the right to participate in democratic institutions could be utilized to expand public involvement in environmental governance. Second generation rights requiring government intervention are also a natural source of inspiration for providing a certain level of environmental quality to citizens of a state. While Sax seems to favor the approach taken by second generation rights (e.g., requiring government action) and analogizes the protection of environmental rights to a welfare-state ideology, he acknowledges the important role played by first generation rights (mainly procedural rights such as the right to information and the right to participate in decision-making) in guiding the search for environmental rights and promoting good democratic values.

Churchill (1996) infers the presence of environmental rights in treaties such as the ICCPR, European Convention, and American Convention by exploring the logical connections between substantive rights and environmental protection. For instance, he reasons that the right to life holds certain promise as an avenue for the protection of environmental rights despite the paucity of successful attempts (at the time of writing) to make such a claim. Another substantive premise for evincing environmental rights, Churchill argues, may originate from the right to be free from interference with one's home and property. While all three treaties listed above contain some provision dealing with this particular right, cases pertaining to this issue have only been brought under the European Convention, mainly on the issue of noise pollution. Yet, at least in the European context, jurists have construed noise pollution as more directly relevant to the right to respect for privacy and family life, or as a kind of environmental pollution that infringes upon individual wellbeing (Pedersen 2008).

In addition to discussing the application of the right to freedom of information to environmental causes, Churchill (1996) also describes the potential for safeguarding environmental rights in the ICESCR, European Social Charter, and American Convention through creative interpretation of the rights to a decent working environment, decent living conditions, and health. He concludes by noting that derivative rights related to environmental protection have been invoked only infrequently, "therefore [reinforcing] the doubts about the usefulness of human rights treaties as a means of protecting the environment" (Churchill 1996, p.108).

International environmental rights

Since their emergence in the 1970s, environmental rights have become entrenched in various legal documents at different levels of governance. At the international level, the 1972 Declaration of the United Nations Conference on the Human Environment (Stockholm Declaration) represents the first major instrument of international law to assert a connection between human rights and environmental protection.[7] The agreement states, "[b]oth aspects of man's environment, the natural and the man-made, are essential to his well-being and to the enjoyment of basic human rights—even the right to life itself" (Stockholm Declaration). Principle 1 of the Stockholm Declaration more closely approximates the human–environment relationship in terms of fundamental rights while also placing the onus on man to preserve the environment: "Man has the fundamental right to freedom, equality and adequate conditions of life, in an environment of a quality that permits a life of dignity and well-being and he bears a solemn responsibility to protect and improve the environment for present and future generations" (Stockholm Declaration). The particular phrasing used in the Stockholm Declaration establishes an environmental right as a derivative of the broader "right to life." However, despite the deliberate use of fundamental rights language, Principle 1 does not formally proclaim a separate solidarity right such as the right to a healthy environment. Instead, the statement suggests that a healthy environment is "necessary to enjoy other basic human rights" (Atapattu 2002, p.74).

The 1982 World Charter for Nature (Charter) followed on the heels of the Stockholm Declaration. The Charter not only sets forth procedural environmental rights,[8] but it also stands "unique in that it is the first, and so far the only, of its kind which recognizes the rights of nature, distinct from the rights of human beings" (Atapattu 2002, p.75). Thus, the Charter remains the sole, widely endorsed international legal document espousing an eco-centric perspective on environmental rights.

In 1992 the international community again emphasized the inextricable link between humans and the environment in which they exist with the Rio Declaration on Environment and Development (Rio Declaration), the centerpiece of international environmental law at the United Nations Conference on Environment and Development. While not couching environmental rights explicitly in the language of fundamental rights, the agreement promoted the idea that human beings "are entitled to a healthy and productive life in harmony with nature" (Rio Declaration). In addition, the Rio Declaration recognized third generation rights such as the right to development and procedural environmental rights.[9]

Finally, after initially being appointed Special Rapporteur to the UN Sub-Commission on Prevention of Discrimination and Protection of Minorities in 1990 and releasing three progress reports, Ms. Fatma Zohra Ksentini submitted her final report on human rights and the environment in 1994. Although not an international agreement, the Ksentini Final Report has provided an influential voice in the global dialogue on human rights and the environment. In particular, the Draft Declaration of Principles on Human Rights and the Environment (Draft Declaration) that accompanies her written report has earned widespread praise among legal scholars (e.g., Popović 1996a). Many of the principles in the Draft Declaration directly recognize procedural and fundamental environmental rights.[10]

While Ksentini intended for the Draft Declaration to "serve as a basis for the United Nations to adopt a set of norms consolidating the right to a satisfactory environment" (Dommen 1998, p.33), her recommendations have not galvanized support in the international arena for a global treaty on environmental rights. Still, her work remains at the forefront of scholarly debates about the legal basis for the protection of environmental rights.[11] More generally, analysts continue to argue over the degree of legal authority vested in this and other documents that seek to codify environmental rights at the international level.[12]

The effort to enact environmental rights at the international level enjoyed renewed interest in March 2012, when the UN Human Rights Council (HRC) passed Resolution 19/10. This resolution established a three-year mandate to study human rights obligations related to the environment, identify best practices in this area, and develop recommendations for working toward the achievement of the Millennium Development Goals (MDGs), especially Goal 7 ("Ensure Environmental Sustainability"). Four months later, the HRC appointed John Knox, a law professor at Wake Forest University School of Law, as the inaugural Independent Expert on Human Rights and the Environment. In March 2015, the HRC reemphasized its commitment to environmental rights by naming Professor Knox Special Rapporteur and extending the mandate another three years.[13] During Knox's tenure as Independent Expert and Special Rapporteur he has participated in numerous consultations, conducted country visits to Costa Rica and France, produced three major reports focused on scoping, mapping, and identifying good practices in the implementation of environmental rights, and launched a website, the Environmental Rights Database,[14] designed to disseminate good practices in the use of human rights to protect the environment. The explicit shift from initially studying the nature and extent of environmental rights to formulating practical ways of realizing these rights signals the UN system's maturing commitment to further developing this relatively new area within international human rights law.

Regional developments

In addition to the international legal sources described above, there are two major regional instruments that pertain to human rights and environmental protection.[15] The 1981 African Charter on Human and Peoples' Rights (African Charter) has earned acclaim for its status as "the first binding instrument, albeit regional, to explicitly endorse the fundamental right to a clean environment" (Atapattu 2002, p.87). The main provision of interest, Article 24, specifically states that "[a]ll peoples shall have the right to a general satisfactory environment favourable to their development" (African Charter). However, the African Charter lacks a definitive articulation of obligations states have when implementing the agreement, and thus it falls somewhere between conventional international law and a declaration in terms of its actual legal authority (Hodkova 1991, p.76).

The 1988 Additional Protocol to the American Convention on Human Rights (Protocol of San Salvador) represents another significant regional instrument that includes environmental rights. Article 11 of the Protocol of San Salvador deals explicitly with environmental rights: "(1) Everyone shall have the right to live in a healthy environment and to have access to basic public services. (2) The State Parties shall promote the protection, preservation and improvement of the environment" (Protocol of San Salvador). This formulation of environmental rights provides for both a solidarity environmental right and a public policy statement mandating a positive duty to be carried out by participating states. Interestingly, the environmental right is qualified by the addition of the phrase "to live," which serves to link the provision to the broader substantive right to life. However, implementation of this regional environmental right is frustrated by the fact that Article 19(6) of the Protocol does not permit individual claimants to bring cases directly to the Inter-American Court of Human Rights on the basis of an alleged violation of one's environmental rights.

If the experiences from these regional agreements offer any indication, such progressive attempts to establish environmental rights at the regional level will likely have little impact in domestic legal systems. Despite efforts to insert third generation environmental rights into these regional agreements, these provisions have been utilized sparingly, if at all.[16] One scholar speculates that few cases from Africa and Latin America have invoked these rights because "there are other preoccupations and priorities when utilizing human rights treaties than protecting the environment" (Churchill 1996, p.108). Regardless of the reason these rights go under-utilized, regional instruments have proven thus far no more viable as effective legal mechanisms for the protection of environmental rights than have international agreements with similar provisions.[17]

Despite the infrequent use of regional treaties in cases involving the protection of environmental rights at the domestic level, regional human rights bodies continue to address issues pertaining to human rights and the environment. The IACHR has been quite active on this front. For example, the IACHR has emphasized in a report on human rights in Ecuador that "[c]onditions of severe environmental pollution, which may cause serious physical illness, impairment and suffering on the part of the local populace, are inconsistent with the right to be respected as a human being" (IACHR 1997).[18] Again, the language used in this report, while suggestive, does not firmly establish a constitutional environmental right, but instead locates an environmental right under the banner of the more universal "right to life and human dignity." Still, while not a binding legal document, this IACHR report and others dealing with environmental rights contribute to a growing cognizance within the region that environmental quality, especially when it impacts human health, falls within the ambit of human rights.

Developments at the state level

When enshrined in national constitutions, environmental rights provisions most often appear phrased as fundamental rights or statements of public policy (Brandl & Bungert 1992). Fundamental rights grant "individual[s] a subjective, or personal, guarantee" to the basic conditions necessary to live a dignified life (Brandl & Bungert 1992, p.9). Unlike statements of public policy, fundamental rights "enjoy the highest level of legal norms, are less subject to political whims, and tend to be better understood by both the polity and citizenry" (May 2005, p.118). Therefore, a fundamental *environmental* right invokes a state's guarantee of the highest legal order assuring an individual of his or her protection from environmental harm.[19] Of those countries that have addressed the environment in their constitutions, a subset has promulgated an environmental right of the fundamental variety, and even fewer have been found to be directly enforceable in domestic legal systems.[20] However, analyzing data from Brazil, Colombia, Costa Rica, Europe, and India, Boyd (2012, p.241) finds that "the majority of lawsuits based on the constitutional right to a healthy environment are successful."

Second, states may include environmental rights in their respective constitutions in the form of a statement of public policy. Such constitutional pronouncements feature "directives and guidelines for governmental action or objective state goals" (Brandl & Bungert 1992, p.16). Statements of public policy typically involve "mandates to the legislature obligating the legislature to regulate specific areas" or "guidelines for the state which address not only the legislature, but also the judicial and executive branches of government" (Brandl & Bungert 1992, p.17). However, statements of public policy wield less legal authority than constitutional environmental rights. In particular, these provisions "are not enforceable by citizens who are aggrieved by environmental degradation" (May 2005, p.116), thus limiting their potential efficacy as a tool for addressing environmental grievances. For instance, China's constitution contains a statement of public policy regarding the state's role in safeguarding the environment: "The state protects and improves the living environment and the ecological environment, and prevents and controls pollution and other public hazards" (Xianfa, ch. I, art. 26 (1982)). Importantly, this article appears in the "General Principles" chapter of the constitution as opposed to the following chapter on "The Fundamental Rights and Duties of Citizens," indicating that the statement does not possess the legal authority normally accorded to human rights.

To clarify, while constitutional environmental rights phrased as fundamental rights confer personal, often enforceable rights that individuals may utilize to bring a complaint of an environmental nature to court, statements of public policy describe guidelines for governmental action but they are not individually enforceable. In terms of characterizing the practical implications of constitutional environmental rights, the exact language used in national constitutions "falls somewhere along a continuum between the subjective fundamental right at one extreme, and the objective statement of public policy at the other" (Brandl & Bungert 1992, p.18). A textual analysis of 142 national constitutions demonstrates that no two environmental rights provisions are worded exactly the same and younger constitutions tend to have a stronger legal framework for the protection of environmental rights (Jeffords 2011). Thus, the potential usefulness of a given constitutional environmental right varies according to its textual construction.

The extent to which constitutions across the world contain environmental rights remains an unsettled empirical inquiry. The quest to produce a universally accepted catalog of all existing constitutional environmental rights has proven elusive because of important differences regarding how these rights are constructed (e.g., a healthy environment versus a safe environment), where they are located within constitutions (e.g., fundamental rights chapter versus the preamble), whether or not limiting language is present (e.g., right may not be claimed in court versus it is directly enforceable), and what types (e.g., procedural versus solidarity) should be included in the count. However, despite these complications, scholars have endeavored to capture the pervasiveness of these rights. Jeffords (2011) finds that 60 national constitutions feature a direct right to the environment. Boyd (2012) concludes that 86 countries have similarly enacted a constitutional environmental right of the solidarity sort. May and Daly (2015) observe that 75 states possess constitutional environmental rights. While the U.S. Constitution does not contain any environmental rights provisions,[21] eight states have enshrined such rights within their respective constitutions.[22]

Direct articulations of environmental rights found within domestic constitutions constitute only one way in which states have sought to protect the human rights of individuals or groups exposed to environmental harms. Other states have found environmental rights through creative judicial interpretation of existing fundamental rights. In India, for example, justices of the Supreme Court have ruled that a "right to a wholesome environment" exists under the fundamental right to life guaranteed by Article 21 of the Indian Constitution.[23] While fundamental environmental rights and public policy statements appear in a significant number of constitutions, only a dozen or so states have located an environmental right under the umbrella of broader constitutional rights, implying the existence of "derivative" environmental rights (May & Daly 2015, p.109).[24]

To summarize, there are two main ways in which fundamental environmental rights have been integrated into domestic constitutional law with the explicit purpose of protecting the rights of individuals or groups where environmental issues are concerned—constitutional environmental rights and environmental rights found by judges to exist under fundamental rights.[25] The first type is present in the form of a potentially functional, though not necessarily self-executing,[26] right within a given constitution, whereas the second type is actively established by judges seeking to expand the purview of existing rights relating to citizens and their natural surroundings. Some examples will no doubt prove illustrative.

In terms of justiciable (e.g., legally actionable) constitutional environmental rights, Angola's constitution presents a suitable example: "Everyone has the right to live in a healthy and unpolluted environment and the duty to defend and preserve it" (Angola Const., ch. II, § I, art. 39(1)). This environmental right appears in Part II of the Constitution, "Fundamental Rights and Duties," and is followed by both a statement of public policy regarding the environment and the stipulation that acts contrary to the state goal of conservation are punishable by law. With regards to environmental rights interpreted by judges to fall under the larger scheme of fundamental rights, India serves as a prime exemplar. In *Subhash Kumar*, the Court held that Article 21 of the Indian constitution, which guarantees the right to life, "includes the right of enjoyment of pollution-free water and air for full enjoyment of life."[27] Both of these examples serve to highlight instances in which environmental rights have been included among the corpus of rights at the state level, providing individuals and groups with legitimate legal avenues for pursuing litigation involving humans and the environment they inhabit.

The year 1974 marked the first time in history that a country adopted a constitutional environmental right. Entrenched in the Constitution of the Socialist Federal Republic of Yugoslavia, this provision read:

> Working people and citizens, organizations of associated labour, socio-political communities, local communities and other self-managing organizations and communities shall have the right and duty to assure conditions for the conservation and improvement of the natural and man-made values of the human environment, and to prevent or eliminate harmful consequences of air, soil, water or noise pollution and the link, which endanger these values and imperil the health and lives of people.
>
> (SFR Yugo. Const., pt. two, ch. I, § 11, art. 87 (1974))

While the percentage of national constitutions featuring provisions related to environmental protection has grown steadily since the 1850s (Ginsburg 2009), the number of states with constitutional environmental rights in particular has expanded dramatically since that watershed moment in 1974 (see Figure 1.1).

Interestingly, the majority of countries with constitutional environmental rights are found in developing countries (May 2005), specifically those

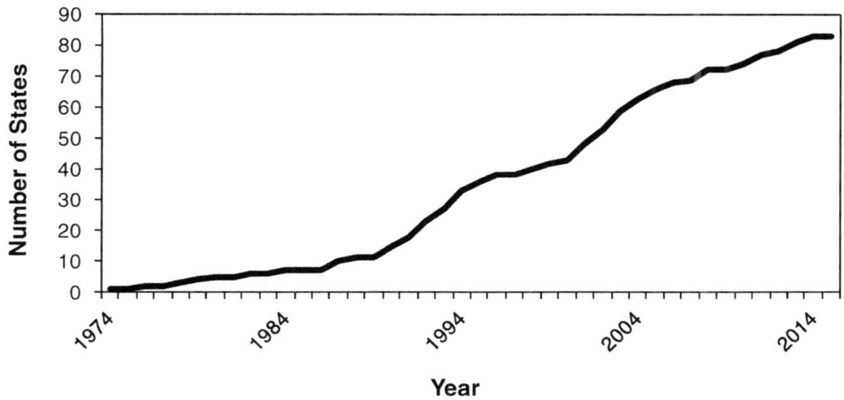

Figure 1.1 Number of states with constitutional environmental rights, 1974–2015

in Europe and Central Asia, Latin America and the Caribbean, and Sub-Saharan Africa (Gellers 2012, p.529).[28] Developing countries, some argue, seem less likely to adopt constitutional environmental rights due to the numerous social, political, and economic problems they face that might take precedence over environmental concerns (Brandl & Bungert 1992, p.84). Especially in the case of post-communist states, the various development issues encountered may cause leaders to concentrate efforts on solving economic problems, effectively diminishing the political will to address environmental problems (Bándi 1992, p.442). However, as the map below indicates (Figure 1.2), constitutional environmental rights are found not only in developing states, but in virtually every continent around the world.

Controversies

This section addresses two main controversies in the literature on environmental rights: (1) how should environmental rights be phrased? and (2) is a human rights approach to environmental protection intrinsically anthropocentric (e.g., human centered)? First, in terms of phrasing environmental rights, constitutions throughout the world display a broad array of linguistic variations, from the common "right to a healthy environment" (Chad Const., tit. II, ch. 1, art. 47 (1996))[29] to the rarer and ambiguously qualified "right to a favourable environment" (Slovak Const., pt. two, ch. six, art. 44, § 1 (2001)) to the uncommon and holistically oriented "[a]ll persons are entitled to an ecologically balanced environment" (Brazil Const., tit. VIII, ch. VI, art. 225 (1988)), with many shades in

Figure 1.2 Current global distribution of countries with constitutional environmental rights

Note: Dark gray denotes countries with constitutional environmental rights.

between. However, the linguistic form that an environmental right takes in a constitution has important ramifications for those who may seek to invoke the right.[30]

On this note, scholars seem to agree that the phrasing of an environmental right should reflect an emphasis on human health, but they diverge on the precise language that should be employed to achieve this end. For instance, one writer advocates in favor of the right to a *safe* environment, arguing that "a narrow formulation focusing exclusively on human health and safety has the best chance of gaining acceptance as a genuine human right" (Nickel 1993, p.284). Another analyst asserts that "[w]ith regard to the parameters of the right, it is submitted that the right to a *healthy* environment provides the better formulation" (Atapattu 2002, p.111). Whereas a safe environment refers more directly to an established level of acceptable risk to human health, a healthy environment is more ambiguous while potentially allowing claimants to benefit from greater flexibility. As a proponent of the right to a healthy environment explains, "[c]laimants need only establish that the activity in question resulted in creating an unhealthy environment for him/her to live in. They do not need to establish damage to their health or well-being at that point" (Atapattu 2002, p.111). Thus, while scholars disagree about the proper linguistic phrasing, they agree that the way in which an environmental right is articulated may have important implications for those seeking protection under the law.

Variation in phrasing may reflect local interpretations of international norms and affect the likelihood of implementation. For instance, phrasing the provision in terms of a right to a safe environment may help potential victims of severe polluting activities by providing a right that is broad enough at the international level to afford individual states the ability to interpret the right according to national regulatory standards. Ultimately, the environmental legacies (Gravelle 1997, p.633), regional influences (Go 2003), and legal traditions (Bruch et al. 2001, p.135) of different states may impact their decision to support one particular formulation of an environmental right over another. The precise language used to enshrine an environmental right in a state constitution may generally reflect the trend toward enactment of environmental rights at the international level while textual differences may speak to the demands and experiences of the domestic context.[31]

Second, some scholars argue that human rights approaches to environmental protection are inherently anthropocentric while others assert that environmental rights, by virtue of their broad formulations, apply to human and non-human entities alike. Similar to the previous controversy, the linguistic form in which the environmental right appears can affect its application. For instance, when written as the right to a safe environment, environmental rights espouse a firmly anthropocentric character, as safety is likely to be defined in terms of risk levels pertinent to humans. It stands to reason, then, that the right to a safe environment "does not speak directly to issues such as biodiversity, the claims of animals, conservation, or sustainable development" (Nickel 1993, p.283). In general, analysts seem to recognize that the endeavor to codify environmental rights is inevitably anthropocentric to some degree (Redgwell 1996, p.86). Yet, this has not stopped others from contending that a creative reinterpretation of law must occur in order to address environmental problems of global scale, and environmental rights in particular must transcend their exclusive focus on humans by extending protection to all relevant ecological beings (Grant et al. 2013, pp.963–964).

The processes of conceptualizing, formulating, ratifying, implementing, enforcing, and interpreting environmental rights are inescapably human-directed activities. However, accepting this fact does not necessarily mean that environmental rights borne out of the human rights tradition need forsake the protection of other forms of life. Some observers speculate that certain formulations of environmental rights may have "a fortuitous spill-over effect to non-humans" (Redgwell 1996, p.87). One writer argues that the mutual co-constitution of man and nature, already recognized in international environmental law,[32] negates the charge of anthropocentrism because "it is impossible to separate the interests of mankind from the protection of nature" (Shelton 1991, p.109). Further, even while mankind may be the intended beneficiary of environmental rights, "[a]t the basic level, the goal [of an environmental right] is to guarantee an environment free from contamination, along with the protection of fauna and flora" (Gormley 1990, p.86).

Environmental rights may also benefit more than just humanity in the long run, as they "may play a useful, but limited role, in the development of an ecological consciousness—one which will foster the adoption of a new environmental ethic" (Taylor 1997, p.311). In this sense, environmental rights developed initially to serve the interests of mankind may promote greater environmental awareness and inculcate in future generations a new set of more holistic environmental values that will ultimately move popular sentiment from anthropocentricism to eco-centrism. Finally, international environmental law has already "breached" the "dam of anthropocentrism," resulting in the development of international norms in which "[a]nimals and nature are unlikely simply to be ignored" (Redgwell 1996, p.87). Therefore, while to a certain extent the enterprise of environmental rights is necessarily anthropocentric, this fact by no means limits the ability of environmental rights to provide protection, directly or indirectly, to the larger ecological system.

Overview of the book

This introductory chapter has elucidated the conceptual and historical foundations of constitutional environmental rights. The remainder of the book pushes current knowledge on the subject further through a discussion of theory and empirics focused on determining the factors that have contributed to the global emergence of environmental rights in national constitutions. Chapter 2 seeks to explain the diffusion of constitutional environmental rights by drawing on insights from international relations (IR) theory, world society theory, and constitutional design theory. I posit that understanding the expansion of constitutional environmental rights offers new evidence regarding the extent to which self-interest or international norms influence state behavior, especially environmental policy-making. The chapter concludes with the presentation of a "world cultural framework of constitutional environmental rights," the first effort to provide an interdisciplinary causal explanation for the proliferation of constitutional environmental rights.

Chapter 3 reports the findings of a global statistical analysis that represents the most comprehensive and theoretically driven attempt to analyze the emergence of constitutional environmental rights to date. Incorporating observations from international relations, sociology, and law, I test several possible explanations for this global trend. I argue that international norms are more important than domestic politics or self-interest in explaining the phenomenon observed. The results largely confirm this hypothesis, but not without adding a layer of complexity to the causal story that motivates the need to employ a more fine-grained analysis designed to tease out the role of contextual factors.

Chapter 4 uses the results of the quantitative analysis to identify a pair of countries, Nepal and Sri Lanka, that share characteristics determined to affect the likelihood of adopting environmental rights, yet experience different constitutional outcomes. Through a qualitative analysis of interviews, and an examination of primary and secondary sources, the comparative case study reveals factors absent from the statistical model that help to explain the apparently divergent paths taken by Nepal and Sri Lanka. The cases support the causal sequence described by the world cultural framework of constitutional environmental rights and strengthen my argument about the importance of norms in the process of adopting environmental rights. This chapter offers the first in-depth comparative assessment chronicling the emergence of environmental rights in the context of designing a national constitution.

Chapter 5 clarifies how the lessons gleaned from the quantitative and qualitative analyses improve our understanding of the emergence of constitutional environmental rights and demonstrate how the journey of environmental rights relates to major questions in international relations. More broadly, I explain how this project has forged new ground in the study of constitutional environmental rights by moving beyond normative debates and anecdotal developments in case law (the first wave of research in this area) and comprehensive efforts to describe and categorize such rights around the world (the second wave of research in this area) into the realm of systematic analyses of the expansion of environmental rights using social science methods and theory. The chapter concludes by offering practical advice regarding the adoption and implementation of environmental rights, and outlining directions for future research.

Conclusion

This introductory chapter has explored the topic of constitutional environmental rights and the puzzle concerning their widespread adoption, reviewed definitions and forms of environmental rights, offered a brief history of developments at the international, regional, and state levels, discussed two areas of controversy surrounding environmental rights, and charted the course through the remainder of this book. The next chapter weaves together elements of IR theory, world society theory, and constitutional design theory in the service of constructing an interdisciplinary theoretical framework for explaining the worldwide expansion of constitutional environmental rights.

Notes

1 For a comprehensive review of litigation involving procedural rights in the environmental rights context, see Shelton (2006, pp.132–163) and May & Daly (2015, pp.251–253).

2 These countries are: Albania, Argentina, Austria, Azerbaijan, Belarus, Bolivia, Brazil, Burkina Faso, Chile, Colombia, Costa Rica, Czech Republic, Ecuador, Ethiopia, France, Georgia, Latvia, Moldova, Montenegro, Norway, Poland, Portugal, Russian Federation, Serbia, Slovak Republic, Thailand, Ukraine, and Venezuela.

3 The right to life has been connected to environmental protection in several domestic legal systems, including Bangladesh, Colombia, Costa Rica, Ecuador, India, Nepal, Pakistan, and Tanzania. See Bruch et al. (2001, pp.164–174).

4 While Gormley (1990) finds promise in conceptualizing environmental rights in terms of solidarity and advocates in favor of merging all three generations of human rights to address environmental protection, Boyle (1996) expresses serious doubts about the utility of defining environmental rights as solidarity rights. See Boyle (1996, p.59).

5 *Robinson Township v. Commonwealth of Pennsylvania*, 83 A.3d 901, 999–1000 (Pa. 2013).

6 The ICESCR and the ICCPR would only enter into force nearly a decade later on January 3, 1976 and March 23, 1976, respectively.

7 Some scholars recognize at least two earlier international actions that contributed to the growing international consideration of the nexus between human rights and environmental protection. Thorme (1991, p.303) contends that "[t]he idea of environment as a human right first emerged in the international arena in 1968 when the General Assembly of the United Nations recognized that technological changes could threaten the fundamental rights of human beings" in a UN General Assembly resolution. Gormley (1990) identifies the Council of Europe's Conservation Year in 1970 as an important precursor to the Stockholm Declaration, albeit with less international participation. See Gormley (1990, p.98).

8 The instrument stipulates, "All persons, in accordance with their national legislation, shall have the opportunity to participate, individually or with others, in the formulation of decisions of direct concern to their environment, and shall have access to means of redress when their environment has suffered damage or degradation" (Charter).

9 Specifically, procedural environmental rights were enumerated in Principle 10 of the Rio Declaration: "Environmental issues are best handled with participation of all concerned citizens, at the relevant level. At the national level, each individual shall have appropriate access to information concerning the environment that is held by public authorities, including information on hazardous materials and activities in their communities, and the opportunity to participate in decision-making processes. States shall facilitate and encourage public awareness and participation by making information widely available. Effective access to judicial and administrative proceedings, including redress and remedy, shall be provided" (Rio Declaration).

10 For a list of the principles included in the Ksentini Report, see Gellers (2012, pp.541–543).

11 Compare Atapattu's (2002) general skepticism (e.g., asserting that "the basic premise on which her reports [sic] is based seems flawed" (p.79)) with Popović's (1996a) commendation (e.g., calling the Final Report "a milestone in advancing protection of human rights and the environment" (pp.491–492)).

12 Compare Gormley's (1990) assertion that the 1972 Stockholm Declaration constitutes customary international law, and that "such 'soft law' is evolving into binding customary international norms" (pp.98, 115) with Atapattu's (2002) negative assessment of the bindingness of the Draft Declaration (p.97)

and May's (2005) contention that both the Stockholm and Rio Declarations are unenforceable (p.122).

13 For more information regarding John Knox's work under the UN Mandate on Human Rights and the Environment, see www.srenvironment.org.

14 See http://environmentalrightsdatabase.org/.

15 Other regional treaties do mention environmental rights, but issues regarding their bindingness and/or jurisprudential impact arguably preclude them from consideration among the most influential regional human rights instruments. Asia does not have a binding regional treaty on environmental rights, but ten members of the Association of Southeast Asian Nations (ASEAN) have signed onto the ASEAN Human Rights Declaration, which includes a "right to a safe, clean and sustainable environment" (ASEAN 2012). The Arab world adopted a binding international treaty, the Arab Charter on Human Rights, that features an environmental right under Article 38: "Every person has the right ... to a healthy environment" (Al-Midani & Cabanettes 2006, p.159). However, observers have criticized this human rights treaty on the grounds that, *inter alia*, it lacks an effective enforcement mechanism such as an Arab Court of Human Rights (Al-Midani 2008). Europe has yet to develop a regional treaty that specifically articulates a binding legal obligation to protect solidarity environmental rights, although the 1990 draft Charter on Environmental Rights and Obligations composed by the United Nations Economic Commission for Europe (UNECE) marked a step in that direction by "[affirming] the universal right to an environment adequate for general health and well-being, as well as the responsibility to protect and conserve the environment for present and future generations" (Taylor 1997, p.348). Also see Shelton (2006, p.166).

16 There is at least one notable instance in which a regional instrument was utilized successfully to provide a justiciable environmental right. Under the instruction of the African Commission on Human and Peoples' Rights in *Communication 155/96—The Social and Economic Rights Action Centre and Another v. Nigeria*, Nigerian courts were authorized to recognize Article 24 of the African Charter. Since then Article 24 has been successfully invoked in Nigeria in the case of *Gbemre v. Shell*. See Ebeku (2007).

17 The Convention on Access to Information, Public Participation in Decision-Making and Access to Justice in Environmental Matters (Aarhus Convention), a treaty established among members of UNECE in 1998, entails several procedural environmental rights, but does not go as far as to create a binding commitment to protect individual or group environmental rights at the regional level, instead couching state obligations in the form of a public policy statement.

18 For a fuller discussion of environmental rights in the context of regional human rights bodies, see Hill et al. (2003, pp.379–381).

19 Throughout this book, environmental rights appearing in national constitutions that are phrased as fundamental rights (e.g., solidarity environmental rights) will simply be referred to as "constitutional environmental rights," notwithstanding the other types of environmental rights identified earlier (e.g., procedural and substantive environmental rights). I have elected to focus on solidarity environmental rights due to their pervasiveness among national constitutions, which enables quantitative analysis and greater analytical consistency than would be achievable by comparing environmental rights designed to accomplish different objectives.

20 May surmises that "of the 130 constitutions that address the environment, only about 60 grant individuals what may be fairly characterized as a fundamental right to a 'clean,' 'healthful,' or 'favorable' environment. More importantly, of

these 60, only a handful have earned judicial imprimatur as being enforceable by affected individuals" (May 2005, p.114).

21 From the late 1960s through the late 1980s, several attempts were made to codify environmental rights in the U.S. either by constitutional amendment or statute. However, all such efforts ultimately failed. For a discussion of the history of these efforts, see Brooks (1992, pp.1068–1070).

22 These states are: Alaska, Hawai'i, Illinois, Massachusetts, Montana, Pennsylvania, Rhode Island, and Texas. For a listing of the exact language of the state constitution environmental rights provisions, see Popović (1996b, p.356).

23 These judgments occurred in *Subhashkumar v. State of Bihar*, AIR 1991 SC 420 and in *Attakoya Thangal v. Union of India*, 1990 (1), KLT 580. See Dias (1994, p.246).

24 Boyd (2012) writes that at least 12 countries have undertaken this approach: Bangladesh, Estonia, Guatemala, India, Israel, Italy, Kenya, Nigeria, Pakistan, Sri Lanka, Tanzania, and Uruguay. As will be discussed in Chapter 4, Nepal also falls into this category. It is interesting to note that of those countries listed, only two—Kenya and Nepal—also have constitutional environmental rights.

25 I exclude procedural and substantive environmental rights from consideration as they do not confer upon individuals the same specific kind of protection regarding environmental matters as do constitutional (e.g., solidarity or third generation) environmental rights. There are also too few cases of either to make generalizable claims. In addition, I also exclude statements of public policy because they are primarily focused on the role of the state in achieving certain policy goals as opposed to being articulated as a positive right guaranteeing citizens a certain level of environmental protection.

26 Indeed, few national constitutions contain what might be considered fully self-executing environmental rights provisions. "To be self-executing, either a provision must expressly state that specific parties have a right to enforce the provision or articulate a clear enough standard so that a court has a law to apply" (Hill et al. 2003, pp.391–392). In addition, provisions found in a Bill of Rights or Fundamental Rights section are said to be justiciable, whereas provisions appearing in a Directive Principles section are not. Therefore, as an example, while Afghanistan's constitution features an environmental rights provision, it is located in the preamble, making the right non-justiciable until further action is taken by the Parliament to define the parameters of the right. For an empirical analysis of the justiciability of constitutional environmental rights, see Jeffords (2011).

27 *Subhash Kumar v. State of Bihar* AIR 1991 SC 420/ 1991 (1) SCC 598.

28 The following is a list of current countries with constitutional environmental rights, by World Bank region: *East Asia and Pacific*—East Timor, Fiji, Indonesia, Mongolia, Philippines, South Korea, Vietnam; *Europe and Central Asia*—Armenia, Azerbaijan, Belarus, Bulgaria, Croatia, Czech Republic, Georgia, Hungary, Kosovo, Kyrgyz Republic, Latvia, Macedonia, Moldova, Montenegro, Romania, Russian Federation, Serbia, Slovak Republic, Slovenia, Turkey, Turkmenistan, Ukraine; *Latin America and the Caribbean*—Argentina, Bolivia, Brazil, Chile, Colombia, Costa Rica, Dominican Republic, Ecuador, Guyana, Jamaica, Mexico, Nicaragua, Paraguay, Peru, Venezuela; *Middle East and North Africa*—Egypt, Iraq, Morocco, Tunisia; *South Asia*—Maldives, Nepal; *Sub-Saharan Africa*—Angola, Benin, Burkina Faso, Cameroon, Cape Verde, Central African Republic, Chad, Côte d'Ivoire, Democratic Republic of Congo, Ethiopia, Guinea, Kenya, Mali, Mauritania, Mozambique, Niger, Republic of Congo, São Tomé and Príncipe, Senegal, Seychelles, South Africa, South

Sudan, Sudan, Togo, Uganda, Zimbabwe; *Western Europe*—Belgium, Finland, France, Greece, Norway, Portugal, Spain.

29 This phrasing, or some close variant, appears in the constitutions of at least 33 countries.

30 As Gravelle (1997) argues, even the choice between the right to a *healthy* environment and the right to a *healthful* environment can have important consequences for potential claimants. See Gravelle (1997, p.637).

31 Go's (2003) characterization of the broader phenomenon of globalizing constitutionalism similarly applies to the universalism versus localism dynamic at play with environmental rights: "it is ... wracked with divergence as much as convergence, a differentiation in content as much as a homogenization in form" (p.90).

32 The World Charter for Nature states that "[m]ankind is a part of nature and life depends on the uninterrupted functioning of natural systems which ensure the supply of energy and nutrients" (Charter).

Bibliography

Additional Protocol to the American Convention on Human Rights in the Area of Economic, Social and Cultural Rights (Protocol of San Salvador), Nov. 14, 1988, art. 11, OASTS No. 69, 28 ILM 156 (1989).

African Charter on Human and Peoples' Rights (African Charter), art. 24, OAU Doc. CAB/LEG/67/3/Rev.5, 21 ILM 58 (1982).

Albania Const., ch. IV, art. 56 (2012).

Al-Midani, M.A., 2008. The Enforcement Mechanisms of the Arab Charter on Human Rights and the Need for an Arab Court of Human Rights. Arab Center for International Humanitarian Law and Human Rights Education. Available at: www.acihl.org/articles.htm?article_id=22 [Accessed July 26, 2016].

Al-Midani, M.A. & Cabanettes, M., 2006. Arab Charter on Human Rights 2004. *Boston University International Law Journal*, 24, pp.147–164.

Anderson, M.R., 1996. Human Rights Approaches to Environmental Protection: An Overview. In A. Boyle & M.R. Anderson, eds. *Human Rights Approaches to Environmental Protection*. Oxford: Clarendon Press, pp.1–23.

Angola Const., ch. II, § I, art. 39(1) (2010).

ASEAN, 2012. ASEAN Human Rights Declaration. Available at: http://aichr.org/?dl_name=ASEAN-Human-Rights-Declaration.pdf [Accessed August 4, 2016].

Atapattu, S., 2002. The Right to a Healthy Life or the Right to Die Polluted? The Emergence of a Human Right to a Healthy Environment Under International Law. *Tulane Environmental Law Journal*, 16, pp.65–126.

Bándi, G., 1992. The Right to Environment in Theory and Practice: The Hungarian Experience. *Connecticut Journal of International Law*, 8, pp.439–466.

Boyd, D.R., 2012. *The Environmental Rights Revolution: A Global Study of Constitutions, Human Rights, and the Environment*, Vancouver, BC: UBC Press.

Boyle, A., 1996. The Role of International Human Rights Law in the Protection of the Environment. In A. Boyle & M.R. Anderson, eds. *Human Rights Approaches to Environmental Protection*. Oxford: Clarendon Press, pp.43–69.

Boyle, A., 2012. Human Rights and the Environment: Where Next? *European Journal of International Law*, 23(3), pp.613–642.

Brandl, E. & Bungert, H., 1992. Constitutional Entrenchment of Environmental Protection: A Comparative Analysis of Experiences Abroad. *Harvard Environmental Law Review*, 16, pp.1–100.

Brazil Const., tit. VIII, ch. VI, art. 225 (1988).

Brooks, R.O., 1992. A Constitutional Right to a Healthful Environment. *Vermont Law Review*, 16, pp.1063–1110.

Bruch, C., Coker, W. & VanArsdale, C., 2001. Constitutional Environmental Law: Giving Force to Fundamental Principles in Africa. *Columbia Journal of Environmental Law*, 26, pp.131–212.

Bruckerhoff, J.J., 2008. Giving Nature Constitutional Protection: A Less Anthropocentric Interpretation of Environmental Rights. *Texas Law Review*, 86(3), pp.615–646.

Chad Const., tit. II, ch. 1, art. 47 (1996).

Churchill, R., 1996. Environmental Rights in Existing Human Rights Treaties. In A. Boyle & M.R. Anderson, eds. *Human Rights Approaches to Environmental Protection*. Oxford: Clarendon Press, pp.89–108.

Dernbach, J.C., May, J.R. & Kristl, K.T., 2015. Robinson Township v. Commonwealth of Pennsylvania: Examination and Implications. *Rutgers University Law Review*, 67, pp.1169–1196.

Dias, A., 1994. Judicial Activism in the Development and Enforcement of Environmental Law: Some Comparative Insights from the Indian Experience. *Journal of Environmental Law*, 6(2), pp.243–262.

Dommen, C., 1998. Claiming Environmental Rights: Some Possibilities Offered by the United Nations' Human Rights Mechanisms. *Georgetown International Environmental Law Review*, 11, pp.1–48.

Ebeku, K.S.A., 2007. Constitutional Right to a Healthy Environment and Human Rights Approaches to Environmental Protection in Nigeria: Gbemre v. Shell Revisited. *Review of European Community & International Environmental Law*, 16(3), pp.312–320.

Ecuador Const., tit. II, ch. 7, art. 71 (2008).

Elkins, Z., Ginsburg, T. & Melton, J., 2009. *The Endurance of National Constitutions*, Cambridge: Cambridge University Press.

Gellers, J.C., 2012. Greening Constitutions with Environmental Rights: Testing the Isomorphism Thesis. *Review of Policy Research*, 29(4), pp.523–543.

Gellers, J.C. & Jeffords, C., 2015. Procedural Environmental Rights and Environmental Justice: Assessing the Impact of Environmental Constitutionalism. *Social Science Research Network*. Available at: http://ssrn.com/abstract=2646739 [Accessed October 1, 2016].

Ginsburg, T., 2003. *Judicial Review in New Democracies: Constitutional Courts in Asian Cases*, Cambridge: Cambridge University Press.

Ginsburg, T., 2009. New Report on Constitutional Treatment of the Environment. *I-CONnect*. Available at: www.iconnectblog.com/2009/11/new-report-on-constitutional-treatment-of-the-environment/ [Accessed July 30, 2016].

Go, J., 2003. A Globalizing Constitutionalism? Views from the Postcolony, 1945–2000. *International Sociology*, 18(1), pp.71–95.

Gormley, W.P., 1990. The Legal Obligation of the International Community to Guarantee a Pure and Decent Environment: The Expansion of Human Rights Norms. *Georgetown International Environmental Law Review*, 3, pp.85–116.

Grant, E., Kotzé, L.J. & Morrow, K., 2013. Human Rights and the Environment: In Search of a New Relationship. Synergies and Common Themes. *Oñati Socio-Legal Series*, 3(5), pp.953–965.

Gravelle, R.K., 1997. Enforcing the Elusive: Environmental Rights in East European Constitutions. *Virginia Environmental Law Journal*, 16, pp.633–660.

Hassan, F., 1983. Solidarity Rights: Progressive Evolution of International Human Rights Law? *New York Law School Human Rights Annual*, 1, pp.51–74.

Hill, B.E., Wolfson, S. & Targ, N., 2003. Human Rights and the Environment: A Synopsis and Some Predictions. *Georgetown International Environmental Law Review*, 16, pp.359–402.

Hodkova, I., 1991. Is There a Right to a Healthy Environment in the International Legal Order? *Connecticut Journal of International Law*, 7, pp.65–80.

Howard, A.E.D., 1996. The Indeterminacy of Constitutions. *Wake Forest Law Review*, 31, pp.383–410.

IACHR, 1997. *Report on the Situation of Human Rights in Ecuador*, OAS doc OEA/Ser.L/V/II.96, doc 10 rev 1, 24 April 1997, 92.

Jeffords, C., 2011. *Constitutional Environmental Human Rights: A Descriptive Analysis of 142 National Constitutions*, The Human Rights Institute, University of Connecticut. Available at: https://ideas.repec.org/p/uct/ecriwp/16.html [Accessed October 1, 2016].

Jeffords, C., 2016. On the Temporal Effects of Static Constitutional Environmental Rights Provisions on Access to Improved Sanitation Facilities and Water Sources. *Journal of Human Rights and the Environment*, 7(1), pp.74–110.

Jeffords, C. & Minkler, L., 2016. Do Constitutions Matter? The Effects of Constitutional Environmental Rights Provisions on Environmental Outcomes. *Kyklos*, 69(2), pp.294–335.

Khilnani, S., Raghavan, V. & Thiruvengadam, A.K., 2013. Reviving South Asian Comparative Constitutionalism. In S. Khilnani, V. Raghavan, & A.K. Thiruvengadam, eds. *Comparative Constitutionalism in South Asia*. New Delhi: Oxford University Press, pp.1–22.

Marks, S.P., 1981. Emerging Human Rights: A New Generation for the 1980s? *Rutgers Law Review*, 33, pp.435–452.

May, J.R., 2005. Constituting Fundamental Environmental Rights Worldwide. *Pace Environmental Law Review*, 23, pp.113–182.

May, J.R., 2013. Constitutional Directions in Procedural Environmental Rights. *Journal of Environmental Law and Litigation*, 28, pp.27–58.

May, J.R. & Daly, E., 2015. *Global Environmental Constitutionalism*, Cambridge: Cambridge University Press.

McClymonds, J.T., 1992. The Human Right to a Healthy Environment: An International Legal Perspective. *New York Law School Law Review*, 37, pp.583–633.

Nickel, J.W., 1993. The Human Right to a Safe Environment: Philosophical Perspectives on its Scope and Justification. *Yale Journal of International Law*, 18, pp.281–295.

Osiatynski, W., 1994. Rights in New Constitutions of East Central Europe. *Columbia Human Rights Law Review*, 26, pp.111–166.

Pedersen, O.W., 2008. European Environmental Human Rights and Environmental Rights: A Long Time Coming? *Georgetown International Environmental Law Review*, 21(1), pp.73–111.

Popović, N., 1996a. In Pursuit of Environmental Human Rights: Commentary on the Draft Declaration of Principles on Human Rights and the Environment. *Columbia Human Rights Law Review*, 27, pp.487–603.

Popović, N., 1996b. Pursuing Environmental Justice with International Human Rights and State Constitutions. *Stanford Environmental Law Journal*, 15, pp.338–376.

Portugal Const., tit. III, ch. II, art. 66(1) (1976).

Redgwell, C., 1996. Life, the Universe and Everything: A Critique of Anthropocentric Rights. In A. Boyle & M.R. Anderson, eds. *Human Rights Approaches to Environmental Protection.* Oxford: Clarendon Press, pp.71–87.

Rehbinder, E. & Loperena, D., 2001. Legal Protection of Environmental Rights: The Role and Experience of the International Court of Environmental Arbitration and Conciliation. *Environmental Policy and Law*, 31(6), pp.282–293.

Sax, J.L., 1990. The Search for Environmental Rights. *Journal of Land Use and Environmental Law*, 6, pp.93–106.

SFR Yugo. Const., pt. two, ch. I, § 11, art. 87 (1974).

Shelton, D., 1991. Human Rights, Environmental Rights, and the Right to Environment. *Stanford Journal of International Law*, 28, pp.103–138.

Shelton, D., 2006. Human Rights and the Environment: What Specific Environmental Rights Have Been Recognized? *Denver Journal of International Law and Policy*, 35, pp.129–171.

Slovak Const., pt. two, ch. six, art. 44, § 1 (2001).

Taylor, P.E., 1997. From Environmental to Ecological Human Rights: A New Dynamic in International Law? *Georgetown International Environmental Law Review*, 10, pp.309–397.

Thorme, M., 1991. Establishing Environment as a Human Right. *Denver Journal of International Law and Policy*, 19(2), pp.301–342.

UN Charter, ch. 1, art. 1, § 3 (1945).

Weston, B.H., 1984. Human Rights. *Human Rights Quarterly*, 6, pp.257–283.

World Charter for Nature (Charter), GA res. 37/7, 37 UN GAOR, Supp. (No. 51) at 17, UN Doc. A/37/51 (1982).

Xianfa, ch. I, art. 26 (1982).

Chapter 2

National constitutions in world society

Introduction

The trend toward constitutional entrenchment of environmental rights, which Boyd (2012) refers to as the "environmental rights revolution," has inspired philosophical debates and numerous efforts to describe and categorize the universe of relevant provisions. Yet, few scholars have sought to provide a systematic explanation for the phenomenon and none has approached the subject from the perspective of international relations. This chapter bridges this theoretical gap and augments the existing understanding of this global development using theory from political science, sociology, and law. First, I discuss how the emergence of constitutional environmental rights relates to major concerns within the field of IR. Second, I demonstrate how IR theory, world society theory, and constitutional design theory each offer useful insights regarding the origins of constitutional environmental rights. Third, I bring together these cognate schools of thought to construct a world cultural framework of constitutional environmental rights.

Constitutional environmental rights and international relations

Literature on constitutional environmental rights has already wrestled with major questions in the field of law (Boyd 2012). But what can a study of constitutional environmental rights teach students of IR? The emergence of constitutional environmental rights relates to three issues of central importance in international relations—the role of the state, the causal significance of norms, and the origins of state preferences. In the space below, I develop a case for the relevance of constitutional environmental rights to IR by describing the relationships between constitutional environmental rights and these areas of concern.

The study of constitutional environmental rights adds a new angle to the discussion in IR literature about the evolving role of the state. While protecting the environment "is a widely recognized public function of the modern state" (Conca 2015, p.108), environmental problems pose a significant challenge to states. Some issues can be managed locally while others require international cooperation. Local environmental problems can become global environmental problems, but some issues "are more global than others" (Yearly 1996, pp.60–61). Environmental flows and transboundary environmental threats that do not respect geographic or political boundaries may constitute a violation of state sovereignty (Kuehls 1998, p.32; Wapner 1998, p.275). Due mainly to industrialization, states increasingly encounter similar environmental issues. Yet, the solutions to these problems are being "rescaled away from the nation-state in multiple directions" (Andonova & Mitchell 2010, p.256).

Does the transboundary nature of environmental degradation spell the end for the state in the domain of environmental governance? On the one hand, actors operating outside the traditional boundaries of the nation-state play a major role in addressing environmental issues. Transnational activists compel states and the international community to take action on environmental problems by engaging in "world civic politics" (Wapner 1995, p.312). Multinational corporations (MNCs) influence the environmental impact of global industry by responding to the demands of consumers throughout the world. Powerful individuals magnify the salience of local environmental issues and spur clean-up efforts (Andonova & Mitchell 2010).

On the other hand, these non-state actors still seek to influence state behavior on environmental concerns, new hybrid forms of governance include states along with outside forces, and states serve as "key broker[s] between international regimes and between global and domestic policy domains" (Compagnon et al. 2012, pp.237–238). Some go as far as to assert that "only the state possesses sufficient authority, legitimacy, resources, and territorial control to enforce environmental rules and norms" (Litfin 1998, pp.3–4). World society theorists in particular remain unapologetically firm about the continued importance of the state in a world premised on legal-rational authority: "where collective societal management is concerned, the state is the only structure that is both responsible and presumably capable" (Boli 1999, p.279).

I contend that the global expansion of constitutional environmental rights simultaneously intrudes state sovereignty and reifies the primacy of the state in environmental governance. First, these rights violate state sovereignty because they reaffirm the hegemonic idea associated with the postwar constitutional paradigm that human dignity is inviolable and the protection of human rights "transcends the history, cultural heritage and social mores of any particular nation-state" (Weinrib 2006, p.90). As a result, the international normative expectation that states will endeavor to protect human rights through domestic legal instruments casts a shadow upon constitution drafters in the modern era (Howard 2009, p.18).[1]

In the current international normative arena, the prerogative to safeguard human rights intersects with the demand for greater environmental protection. This normative collision complicates the modern conception of sovereignty. Sovereignty, some argue, acts as an impediment to ecological protection (Kamieniecki & Granzeier 1998, p.260). However, although states continue to retain sovereignty over their natural resources and their ability to protect them, international norms exert an external pressure on states to manage their human and natural capital according to certain predetermined ways (Litfin 1998, p.1). Environmental rights in particular may possess a normative force all their own, mobilizing support for advocacy efforts across jurisdictions (Conca 2015, p.108). As new norms cause traditional notions of sovereignty to erode, states may find it increasingly difficult to shirk their responsibility to protect the natural environment on the basis of national interest or economic development. Indeed, "environmental ideas have begun the slow process of redefining what it means to be a sovereign state in the ecological era" (Falkner 2012, p.517).

Given the unrivaled rate at which constitutional environmental rights gained recognition in constitutions throughout the world (Boyd 2012, p.76), it seems reasonable to expect that such rights will become regular fixtures among the corpus of rights that states codify. Despite observable variations in national environmental circumstances, constitutional environmental rights are likely to appear in any new governing charter. However, their instantiation cannot be seen purely as an expression of popular sovereignty, a hallmark of liberal constitutionalism (Neuman 2003, p.1866); their origins and the basis of their legitimacy lie at the international level. Thus, it is the legalistic and normative dimensions of constitutional environmental rights, not the environmental dimension, that cause violations of state sovereignty.

Second, constitutional environmental rights also reinforce the centrality of the state in environmental governance because they signal a shift away from locating the solution to environmental problems in global institutions and a move toward establishing the state as the proper authority in environmental matters. Instead of depending largely on activists, political leaders, and scientists to address global environmental issues through a patchwork quilt of issue-specific regimes, environmental concerns increasingly fall within the purview of domestic legal systems, which then take on the tasks of adjudicating violations and articulating the contours of these innovative provisions. Solving environmental crises begins to hinge less on international diplomacy and scientific consensus building and more on domestic legal adversarialism. The enforcement of constitutional environmental rights then lies in the hands of experts (e.g., "administrative rationalism") and the people (e.g., "democratic pragmatism") (Dryzek 2013). Therefore, such rights stand as a rebuttal to the idea, embedded in neoliberal economic thinking, that the state is "too large to manage local environmental problems or too small to address global environmental risks" (Compagnon et al. 2012, p.241). On the contrary, the state is "just right."

Next, constitutional environmental rights present new evidence regarding the extent to which norms matter when assessing state behavior. As argued in the previous chapter, the presence of constitutional environmental rights in the international normative arena both constrains *and* constitutes states. In this sense, constitutional environmental rights reflect both "regulative norms, which order and constrain behavior, and constitutive norms, which create new actors, interests, or categories of action" (Finnemore & Sikkink 1998, p.891). In terms of their capacity to limit the bounds of acceptable state behavior, "constitutions impose constraints upon government and protect the individual's freedoms from arbitrary or abusive state action" (Keith 2002, p.113). Constitutional rights also constrain states in that they contribute, along with other rights provisions, to a cultural "script" (Meyer et al. 1997, p.150) that enumerates the kinds of human rights modern states are expected to adopt. For example, as a wave of constitutionalism spread across the globe following the end of World War II, virtually all constitutions drafted during this period feature the same set of civil and political rights expressed within the Universal Declaration on Human Rights and the International Covenant on Civil and Political Rights (Law 2008, p.11).

A similar dynamic regarding environmental provisions in constitutions written or amended has been observed in more recent times: "while 147 nations added environmental rights and/or responsibilities to their constitutions since the early 1970s, 40 of the remaining 46 nations bypassed the opportunity to do so despite carrying out other constitutional reforms" (Boyd 2012, pp.51–52). These figures support the idea that states increasingly find themselves motivated to enact advanced forms of constitutional environmental protection. Some empirical evidence suggests that in an era of globalization, the prospect that policy convergence will lead to a race to the top (e.g., more stringent policies) as opposed to a race to the bottom (e.g., less stringent policies) seems promising (Law 2008, p.19). However, a meta-analysis of convergence studies points to generally mixed results (Busch et al. 2012, p.201). Still, given the level of textual ambiguity that characterizes most constitutional environmental rights, a fact that may hinder their enforcement but make adoption fairly non-controversial, these provisions are likely to continue to constrain the decisions states make during the constitution drafting process irrespective of the degree to which they are successfully implemented.

But constitutional environmental rights also constitute state identities. By identities, I mean "relatively stable, role-specific understandings and expectations about self" (Wendt 1992, p.397). Since the time of the Industrial Revolution, the world has experienced a paradigmatic shift in the way that people think about nature. Whereas society used to view nature merely as an exploitable resource, now humanity has begun to treat it as a life-sustaining global ecosystem (Frank 1997). This change in cognitive framing has altered the very identity of the nation-state. Indeed, environmental protection has become a central purpose of the state itself (Frank et al. 2000, p.100). Fulfilling this purpose sends a signal that a country takes seriously its duties as a member of the broader international community of states. China, for instance, joined the Cartegena Protocol on Biosafety under the Convention on Biological Diversity in part to "achieve full integration into international society" (Busch et al. 2012, p.207).

In addition, in the wake of World War II, human rights norms have been assigned special importance within this international society. Governments and international organizations sanction states that violate human rights while news outlets "name and shame" human rights abusers (Hafner-Burton & Tsutsui 2005, p.1381; Hafner-Burton 2008, p.689). Meanwhile, states with positive human rights records are identified as "member[s] of the community of liberal states" (Risse & Sikkink 1999, p.8). Those who fail to adhere to the rules of the community are socialized to bring themselves into compliance, a process known as "acculturation" (Goodman & Jinks 2004, p.630). Constitutional environmental rights represent the union of the aforementioned identity markers in international society—environmental protection and safeguarding human rights. A state that adopts these rights sends a signal that its identity conforms to the expectations of the larger normative community.

Finally, constitutional environmental rights breathe new life into discerning the origins of state preferences. As discussed in the previous point, these constitutional provisions entail the legalization of norms relating to environmental protection and human rights. In the course of enacting constitutional environmental rights, the motivation underlying the adoption of one norm may prove more influential than the motivation behind adopting the other. Or perhaps the combination of the two norms invites a complex interaction between different motivating factors. In addition, states may enact norms pertaining to the environment and human rights due to factors internal or external to the state, or for ideational or material reasons, or a combination of these considerations (Drezner 2001, p.57). Table 2.1 depicts potential sources of motivation for norm institutionalization, or the entrenchment of a norm within a "state's

Table 2.1 Sources of motivation for norm institutionalization

		Interests	
		Ideational	*Material*
Focus	*Internal*	Boost national pride	Solicit votes
	External	Join international society	Obtain foreign aid

constitutional, regulative, or judicial systems" (Cortell & Davis 2000, p.70), along with a hypothetical example for each dyad.

I argue, in line with constructivists and world society theorists, that while different sources of motivation may undergird both of these international norms, the result—constitutional convergence—indicates that the global normative environment in which states are immersed holds causal significance all its own. This is not to say that states are deprived of agency, however. States and global norms interact in reciprocal fashion, continuously shaping both the agents and their encompassing structures (Checkel 1998, p.328). Not only will a study of constitutional environmental rights add new wrinkles to the debate about the factors influencing state preferences, but such an undertaking will also venture into the relatively uncharted territory of what I call "blended norms," or combinations of two or more sets of intersubjective expectations about the appropriate behavior of states.

International relations theory: norms, interests, and the state

In this section, I explain how an investigation into the global convergence on constitutional environmental rights might profit from insights offered by IR theory, and, reciprocally, how the resulting knowledge may contribute to queries at the heart of IR scholarship. I begin by considering how major theoretical camps within the field might interpret the development of environmental rights before examining the ways in which IR theorists explain the origins of state behavior. The section closes with a discussion regarding how the proliferation of these rights builds upon previous understandings of the state and state behavior in the international system.

Realists, or those for whom power is the *raison d'être* in international politics, might view the expansion of environmental rights as unimportant so long as power politics continues to dominate the interactions among states. Powerful states, the only actors of consequence in IR for these theorists, will continue to act in their own self-interest (e.g., preserving or increasing relative power) regardless of emerging or existing international laws and norms (Mearsheimer 1994, p.7). Thus, realists would likely maintain that environmental rights will be impotent to change state interests. Liberals, or those for whom international institutions offer the promise of a better world irrespective of power politics considerations (Barkin 2003, p.335), might welcome environmental rights as a logical offshoot of existing institutions and norms that have demonstrated progress in the areas of environmental and human rights protection. Liberals might therefore argue that these rights possess the potential to alter state interests, improve the environment, and help to secure human rights. Finally, Marxists, or those for whom international politics is characterized by a vicious cycle in which powerful capitalist states exploit peripheral industrializing states (Walt 1998, p.32), might view environmental rights with great skepticism. For these scholars, new rights might function as diversionary tactics employed by elites to avoid addressing the underlying cause of environmental degradation and human rights abuses—global capitalism.

Theories of IR that offer a means of understanding the spread of constitutional environmental rights generally advance either normative or rationalist–materialist explanations for state behavior. Normative explanations highlight the importance of international norms in explaining the actions undertaken by states. Here, norms are defined as "shared expectations about appropriate behavior held by a collectivity of actors" (Checkel 1999, p.83). Research in this area has demonstrated that norms have had an independent effect on, *inter alia*, ending apartheid in South Africa (Klotz 1995), changing Japanese attitudes toward immigrant workers (Gurowitz 1999), eradicating the practice of female genital cutting (Boyle et al. 2002), and prohibiting wartime looting of cultural treasures (Sandholtz 2007).

Students of international norms have sought to specify the conditions under which norms emerge and change. Early work by Finnemore & Sikkink (1998) outlines the process through which norms gain influence and produce cognizable outcomes. This "norm life cycle" approach consists of three successive stages—norm emergence, "norm cascade," and norm internalization. Norms first become prominent with the aid of progressive agents of change called "norm entrepreneurs." Next, the pressure to conform to international standards and the desire to earn legitimacy and enhance self-esteem cause a domino effect among states. Finally, norms become regular rules of social and political life, and deviations from them yield scrutiny and punishment. However, the authors cautiously note that not all norms proceed successfully through these three stages on the way to becoming taken for granted.

Building on the aforementioned effort, Risse & Sikkink (1999) explain variation in the implementation of human rights norms using a five-phase "spiral model" in which transnational advocacy networks (TANs) socialize states into incorporating these norms into their domestic practices. TANs refer to "networks of activists, distinguishable largely by the centrality of principled ideas or values in motivating their formation" (Keck & Sikkink 1999, p.89) that engage in the exchange of information and services centered around advancing a particular cause. TANs may effect change proactively by drawing attention to an issue currently unattended to by decision-makers and demanding action, or reactively by compelling compliance with legal obligations already adopted but not adequately implemented and enforced. Risse and Sikkink (1999) argue that while states may initially adopt human rights norms for self-interested reasons, transnational and domestic actors ultimately compel meaningful compliance. This "boomerang" mechanism has been demonstrated empirically by Hafner-Burton & Tsutsui (2005), who dub this phenomenon "the paradox of empty promises." For Risse and Sikkink, norms may originate in international institutions, but they become localized and enforced through the actions of transnational and domestic groups. Scholars of global environmental politics have also emphasized the important role played by transnational and domestic activist groups in effecting environmental policy change at the international, regional, state, and individual levels (Wapner 1995; Raustiala 1997; Betsill & Corell 2001; Gough & Shackley 2001; Ho 2001; Hallstrom 2004).

Sandholtz (2008) develops a cyclical model of international norm change whereby conflicts between different sets of rules result in contestation and eventually the modification of those rules. Importantly, he argues that normative and rational motivations both influence actors, but normative factors are present prior to calculations of self-interest, as they provide the rule structure in which states operate. He finds that his model of norm change aptly describes the evolution of international rules about wartime plunder.

Approaching the topic of norm-making from a socio-legal angle, Halliday (2009) puts forth a recursive model in which four mechanisms—indeterminacy, contradictions, diagnostic struggles, and actor mismatch—characterize a dynamic, interactive process that occurs among global actors, within states, and between states and the international arena. Similar to Finnemore & Sikkink (1998) and Sandholtz (2008), the author couches his framework using the language of norm cycles. In addition, Halliday also offers an explanation that assigns causal significance to both the structure of the normative environment and the agency of transnational and domestic actors. Yet, as a point of departure, this model enriches the discussion of international norms by emphasizing systematic, historical, and comparative dimensions of norm change.

Rationalists (e.g., those who privilege explanations of state behavior that focus on the promotion of self-interest) contend that norms *constrain* behavior to the extent that they impact the incentives actors confront, while constructivists maintain that norms *constitute* identities and interests possessed by actors (Checkel 1997, p.473). Throughout this discussion normative explanations will be associated primarily with a constructivist approach to IR, since the rationalist perspective on norms adheres to an entirely different logic, one in which actors engage in certain behaviors for calculated reasons mainly relating to power or wealth maximization (e.g., the logic of consequences) as opposed to identity and social norms (e.g., the logic of appropriateness). However, the role that norms play in influencing state behavior does not necessarily suggest a strict dichotomy. As one analyst observes, "norms sometimes constrain and sometimes constitute" (Checkel

1997, p.474). Acknowledging the complex reality facing states, I will argue that, in the case of constitutional environmental rights, norms do both.

Thus, normative explanations, as they will be considered in the present review, fall mainly under the purview of a constructivist approach to IR. Constructivism refers to the view that "[a]ctors' interests and preferences are not given outside social interaction or deduced from structural constraints in the international or domestic environment" (Risse & Sikkink 1999, p.8). In the view of constructivists, the determinants of international politics are social, not material, and this social environment "shape[s] actors' identities and interests, rather than just their behavior" (Wendt 1995, pp.71–72). Central to this approach is the notion that the structure of the international system, constituted by ideas and processes, is constantly shaping and being shaped by actors operating within its confines. In this sense, constructivism avoids the charge of being purely macro-structural (e.g., only the system matters) or methodologically individualist (e.g., only scaled-up individual rationality matters). Instead, the mutually constitutive, interactive orientation of the approach falls more in line with sociological structuralism (Wendt 1995, p.73). For constructivists, neither agents nor structures are considered subservient to the other (Checkel 1998, p.326).

The rationalist–materialist camp consists of neorealists and neoliberal institutionalists, both of whom afford international norms limited independent explanatory power. For these scholars, norms operate only as intervening variables between what they deem to be the primary sources of state interests and the behavior observed (Björkdahl 2002, p.11). Neorealists hold that "norms reflect the distribution of power among states" (Florini 1996, p.365) and the outcomes produced by interactions among states "merely reflect the interests and relative strength of the contending parties" (Raymond 1997, p.205). In terms of their ability to impact the international system, norms and institutions "matter only on the margins" (Mearsheimer 1994, p.7). Thus, norms only change when the global distribution of power changes. For example, a neorealist might observe a state changing its behavior in apparent congruence with an international norm and explain the shift in terms of socialization led by a hegemon (Ikenberry & Kupchan 1990).

Neoliberal institutionalists, by contrast, while perhaps assigning greater weight to norms than their neorealist counterparts, similarly reject the argument that ideational factors carry independent explanatory value (Björkdahl 2002, p.11). Scholars in this tradition, concerned mainly with understanding coordination problems and factors that lead to cooperation (Keohane 1984; Axelrod & Keohane 1985; Oye 1985), instead claim that outcomes of import in global affairs, such as the design of international institutions, follow from the rational self-interests of states (Koremenos et al. 2001, p.762). Also similar to the neorealists, analysts approaching the study of IR from this perspective focus on the importance of material interests in explaining state behavior (Kaufmann & Pape 1999, p.640). In the neoliberal institutionalist worldview, international norms and institutions are only instrumental in solving coordination problems to the extent that they "reduce transactions costs and uncertainty or promote sidepayments" (Checkel 1997, p.475). For example, a neoliberal institutionalist might witness the same phenomenon described above and attribute it to rational calculations about the externally bestowed material benefits a state might earn by enacting certain reforms. In both instances, norms are epiphenomenal; that is, their explanatory power is subsumed by more important factors relating to power or wealth.

Although the two perspectives detailed here—those of the normative and rationalist–materialist varieties—have been presented as fairly discrete, some theorists maintain that the reality of state behavior belies such either/or categorization (Klotz 1995, p.13). Some stipulate further that rationality and norms are, in fact, inseparable (Finnemore & Sikkink 1998, p.888). So-called "second generation" research on international environmental politics has demonstrated that there is room for both perspectives at the political science dinner table (Zürn 1998, p.619). While some have anointed the controversy between constructivism and rationalism the main dispute within IR theory (Katzenstein et al. 1998), others stress that the two views are compatible, or, more precisely, that constructivism is not necessarily hostile to (at least classical) realism (Barkin 2003, p.326).

Fearon & Wendt (2002) also contend that rationalism and constructivism are not irreconcilable. They conclude that scholars of both analytical perspectives generally agree that ideas matter in international politics: "[i]n rationalism the main explanatory role of norms is 'regulative' of the behavior of exogenously given agents, whereas in constructivism norms are 'constitutive' of actors' identities and interests in the first place" (Fearon & Wendt 2002, p.61). Ideas are only subjugated where material concerns are deemed to possess *more* explanatory value. Therefore, materialism may be said to more definitively oppose constructivism than does rationalism. The true sticking point within this debate revolves around how to interpret the role (e.g., primary or auxiliary) and locate the basis (e.g., material or social) of power in international politics and determine the conditions under which one set of factors appears to predominate (P.T. Jackson 2004).

While participants in the constructivism–rationalism debate seek to ascertain the determinants of state interests and how they relate to power, no theory alleging to explain state behavior can ignore the relevance of domestic politics in the process of conducting such an inquiry. Traditionally, system-level theorists of IR have treated domestic conditions as "an independent or intervening variable and sometimes an irrelevant one" (Gourevitch 1978, p.881). But analyzing the causal impact of international norms requires understanding how they "actually reach the domestic arena" (Checkel 1997, p.476).

Research on the nexus between international norms and domestic conditions is legion. Legro (1997, p.32) argues that while international norms may have influenced the use of force during World War II, the variation observed among states was due to factors present at the level of national society, mainly the beliefs held by military organizations. Checkel (1999, p.84), embracing norms as intervening variables while not trivializing them, adds that receptiveness to international norms varies according to the kinds of domestic norms and domestic structures present within a state. Gurowitz (1999, p.416) finds that the impact of international norms varies according to a government's views toward the international society that lays claim to the norms and how the norms around an issue area are treated in the realm of domestic politics. Kaufmann & Pape (1999, p.641) identify two mechanisms through which international norms translate into domestic policies—societal diffusion and transnational activism. Cortell & Davis (2000, p.66) illustrate that the adoption of and compliance with norms is contingent upon the extent to which a given norm is internally salient and perceived as legitimate, and characteristics of the domestic structural environment. Acharya (2004) shows that successful norm diffusion is a function of the degree to which local agents can adapt foreign ideas to match their existing beliefs and identities, a process called "congruence building." Halliday (2009) argues that both domestic structures and domestic politics affect state receptiveness to international norms. Ultimately, those who assign domestic factors a great deal of causal weight do so in order to understand whether or not and under what conditions international norms matter. One analyst goes as far as to state that "[i]nternational norms can matter *only* when they are used domestically and when they work their way into the political process" (Gurowitz 1999, p.416; emphasis added).

Domestic factors prove analytically troublesome for scholars advancing a macro-structural explanation for world politics because they introduce considerable variation into an epistemological approach oriented toward obtaining parsimonious, systemic behavioral laws. Including domestic conditions in the conversation about state behavior is further complicated when one considers whether and how international politics influences domestic structures or vice versa, or whether there exist reciprocal interactions between these levels of analysis. At the same time, a focus on the relationship between factors internal to the state and state behavior cannot offer a sufficient explanation for the breathtaking degree of convergence or isomorphism witnessed across the globe (Florini 1996, p.366; Meyer et al. 1997, p.145; Boyle et al. 2002).

Convergence refers to "the tendency of societies to grow more alike, to develop similarities in structures, processes, and performances" (Kerr 1983, p.3). Isomorphism, a cousin to convergence, describes a process that "forces one unit in a population to resemble other units that face the same set of environmental conditions" (DiMaggio & Powell 1991, p.66). Given the inevitable tradeoffs one observes when seeking to capture theoretical parsimony or descriptive complexity, attempts to explain the isomorphic tendencies of states within a given issue area should strive to search for both commonalities across cases that explain convergence and particularities within cases that result in differential responses to the presence of international norms (Arjomand 2000).

While the three approaches examined above—normative, rationalist–materialist, and domestic politics—offer at times competing and potentially complementary explanations for interest formation and state behavior, the subject of constitutional environmental rights compels a discussion about the source of international norms themselves. Where do international norms come from? Theorists from the "English School" (ES) of IR provide useful preliminary insights into this question. ES scholars posit that the structure of the international system is not an external factor that directs state behavior, but rather a social construct that both shapes and is shaped by states (Clark 1999, p.141). Researchers in this tradition refer to this dynamic system as an "international society" (Bull 1977; Bull & Watson 1984). This international society is constituted by a society of states bound by common values (Raymond 1997, p.207). However, analysts disagree about the extent to which ES tips the scale in favor of agentic or structural explanations of international politics. While Brown (2001, p.427) describes the international society as both "state-centric" and situated in a context marked by inter-state relations, Buzan (1993, p.340) claims that the development of international society presupposes the existence of an identifiable world culture.

World society theory: world culture and environmentalization

Answers to questions surrounding the emergence, endurance, and demise of values held by international society are brought into sharper focus by sociological institutionalists, specifically world society theorists. Whereas IR scholars define the contours of the global normative environment through a piecemeal accounting of various international norms that reflect Western "cosmopolitan" ideals (Nadelmann 1990, p.484), world society theorists specify what they consider as the dominant attributes of world culture. As one political scientist summarizes, "[world society theorists] do more than simply argue that social structure matters; they tell us what the social structure *is*" (Finnemore 1996, p.327; emphasis in original). World society's emphasis on explicating the content of the international normative environment, I suggest, proves instructive when trying to understand the reasons for the global expansion of constitutional environmental rights. In support of this assertion, I review world society theory and its major components with an eye toward explaining the expansion of constitutional environmental rights.

World society theory is predicated on the notion that "*[m]any features of the contemporary nation-state derive from worldwide models constructed and propagated through global cultural and associational processes*" (Meyer et al. 1997, pp.144–145; italics in original). For world society theorists, actions by and structures within states exhibit a striking level of similarity despite the presence of vastly different capacities, economies, geographies, histories, and so on. But the explanation for this degree of similarity lies not in functionalist logic (e.g., institutions are created to address specific societal needs). Scholars in the world society camp dispute that institutional isomorphism reflects the tendency of states to adopt common solutions to common problems. Instead, the common factor responsible for the surprising level of uniformity across states is a dominant world culture, defined as "a set of fundamental principles and models, mainly ontological and cognitive in character, defining the nature and purposes of social actors and action" (Boli & Thomas 1999, p.14). International organizations and structures promote the adoption of these models, helping them to achieve a kind of "taken-for-granted" quality (Schofer et al. 2012, p.59). Yet, the preeminence of world culture does not mean that institutions will emerge and change in identical ways. Differences in institutional contexts mean that "specific actions in specific contexts vary almost without limit" (Boli & Thomas 1999, p.18).

World culture is historically contingent (Meyer et al. 1987, p.27), and, although initially derived from a "Western model of a liberal social order" (Lechner 1991, p.1115), it is not solely the product of powerful Western states (Boli & Thomas 1997, p.172). This global culture possesses several main attributes. First, world culture emphasizes *individualism*. The focus on the individual, motivated by the rise of industrialization and urbanization, marks a shift away from traditional cultures and toward the cultivation of personal identities separate from the realm of social organization. This ideology of individualism has emerged in tandem with a "contradictory" development—the designation of the state "as the primary locus of power and authority in society for building progress" (Boli 1987, p.133). Yet, the concurrent establishment of individualism on the one hand and legitimation of the nation-state as the main architect of societal organization and governance in society (Meyer 1987, p.42) on the other has produced a global culture that assigns great importance to the protection of human rights (Elliott 2007, p.344).

Second, world culture entails *rationalization*. That is, aspects of everyday life are organized to achieve collective ends (Meyer et al. 1987, p.24). Rationalization, pursued through means such as science and logic, helps actors to achieve progress (e.g., wealth) and justice (e.g., equality) (Finnemore 1996, p.331; Boli and Thomas 1997, p.181). Third, world culture hinges upon *universalism*. The exogenously given world culture features cultural models that are "presumed to be universally valid" (Boli & Thomas 1997, p.173), resulting in their institutionalization worldwide. This element of world culture helps to explain why similar institutions and policies appear across the globe while local models fail to spread with equal fervor (Meyer et al. 1997, p.149).

The theory of "ecological modernization" (EM) developed in environmental sociology helps to explain how rationalization influences efforts to address environmental concerns in modern society. EM is multi-faceted; it has been employed as a school of thought, a characterization of current environmental discourse, a way of describing private sector behavior that both increases efficiency and reduces environmental harm, and a catch-all term referring to "almost any environmental policy innovation or environmental improvement" (Buttel 2000, p.59). But above all, EM is a social theory that explores the relationship between contemporary environmental challenges and solutions centered on technology, market forces, and the state.

EM features four characteristics. First, it holds that ecological reform will mainly be accomplished though scientific and technological advances. Second, it asserts the importance of the market and economic actors in the process of transforming industrial society to become more environmentally benign. Third, it highlights that this process will necessarily require the state to undergo major changes, such as adopting a proactive stance toward environmental protection, incorporating participatory decision-making procedures, decentralizing environmental governance, and transferring some responsibility to the market. Fourth, it alters the role of the environmental movement from agitator, critic, and resister to ally of those forces and organizations that it formerly opposed (Mol 1997, pp.140–141).

EM offers three important insights regarding the kinds of environmental policy innovations suggested by world society theory and rationalization. First, policies will support the development and diffusion of new, more environmentally friendly technologies intended to replace the old industrial ones. Second, policies will be designed with an eye toward monetizing nature by placing economic value on the environment and the services it provides (Spaargaren & Mol 1992). Third, although policies will tend to mimic those enacted by Western states, important differences may remain due to variation in national institutions (Mol 2002, pp.110–111). Empirical research on the ability of EM to achieve ecological reform is not encouraging, however. Berger et al. (2001) show, for example, that policy outcomes based on an EM approach can fall critically short of expectations due to unforeseen distributional conflicts and a naïve view of the willingness of governments and businesses to change. Still, EM is at least theoretically beneficial in that it illustrates the types of environmental policy innovations that might be observed in a world in which rationalization, and to a lesser extent universalism, are dominant fixtures.

World society theorists have taken particular interest in understanding the reasons for isomorphism in the environmental domain, concluding that global structures often feature more prominently than the particular circumstances of individual states. Frank (1997) concludes that the discursive shift from treating nature as an economic resource to conceiving nature as a scientific ecosystem increased the rate at which international environmental treaties were formed. Frank et al. (2000) analyze the dramatic increase in state activities designed to protect the environment, a development they refer to as "environmentalization." They find that a top-down structural explanation in which environmental protection is considered a basic responsibility of the state proves more statistically compelling than bottom-up domestic explanations focused on environmental degradation and national wealth. Hironaka (2002) observes that the enactment of environmental impact assessment (EIA) legislation in developing countries is more strongly associated with conditions present in the international arena than with factors internal to states. Schofer & Hironaka (2005) empirically demonstrate that the structure, penetration, and persistence of the world environmental regime have reduced levels of global environmental degradation. Frank et al. (2007) determine that environmental policy reform in Asia is driven more by links to world society and the global environmental regime than domestic environmental non-governmental organizations (ENGOs) or local environmental deterioration. Finally, Shandra et al. (2009) surmise that international non-governmental organizations (INGOs), inter-governmental organizations (IGOs), and international environmental treaties (all hallmarks of world society) are positively associated with lower levels of water pollution across the developing world.

Despite the consistent findings issued in these reports, recent research complicates the view that international-level factors matter more than domestic conditions in locating the impetus for organizational change and convergence where environmental issues are at stake. Vasi (2007) obtains evidence that adoption of the Cities for Climate Protection program among local governments resulted from a complex interaction between local, national, and global processes. Jorgenson et al. (2011) conclude that the presence of ENGOs (a proxy for the penetration of world society in a given state) within developing countries reduces deforestation rates, but does not appear to affect levels of greenhouse gas emissions or water pollution caused by manufacturing. Thus, while the balance of the evidence suggests that world society may be responsible for a great deal of isomorphism and environmentalization, the link between international-level structures and environmental quality is not dispositive. In addition, as much of the work in this area relies on large-N quantitative analyses that lack empirically verified causal explanations, the extent to which observed convergences can be confidently claimed as products of a single or multiple levels of social organization has yet to be resolved.

Constitutional design theory: endogenous and exogenous explanations

Scholarship examining determinants of constitutional design choices provides a third area of literature that informs an interdisciplinary approach to understanding the emergence of constitutional environmental rights. In general, the study of constitution making has evolved into two main lines of research, one focused on endogenous (e.g., internal) conditions that shape constitutions and another centered on exogenous (e.g., external) factors that influence decisions about constitution drafting. Below I review both endogenous and exogenous constitutional studies, and describe in greater detail the dynamics that characterize the ways in which constitutional ideas diffuse globally. I leave aside scholarly efforts to prescribe optimal constitutional design (e.g., Lijphart 1991).

Endogenous constitutional studies analyze the domestic determinants of constitutional design and the resulting structure of and content embodied within governing charters. Much of this literature, which stems from the law and economics tradition, emphasizes a microeconomic approach to understanding how rational actors operate under given constraints to devise national constitutions (Buchanan & Tullock 1962). Research in this vein has highlighted the importance of different political models of constitution making (Arato 1995), motivations of the framers (Elster 1995; Acemoglu & Robinson 2000), constitutional bargaining (Brown 2008), societal preferences (Ticchi & Vindigni 2010), and geographical factors (Hayo & Voigt 2010) in explaining the particular institutional arrangements that become entrenched within a constitution.

Exogenous constitutional studies explore the relationship between constitutions and the international context in which they are written in general, and the observable trend toward constitutional convergence in particular. At its broadest level of abstraction, the noticeable convergence across constitutions is seen as a result of "internationalization," a term encompassing the range of consequences that international and supranational institutions, norms, and processes have on domestic constitutions (Saunders 2014). More specifically, scholarship in this area analyzes several types of phenomena which together constitute "transnational constitutionalism" (Yeh & Chang 2008). Transnational constitutionalism describes three global dynamics—the constitutionalization of the international legal arena, the cross-national dialogue of judicial decision-making, and the increasing convergence of national constitutions. Each of these areas will be explored below, with special attention paid to global constitutional convergence.

First, some scholars have argued that certain international institutions, such as regimes or treaties, might be considered constitutions in their own right because they possess constitutional attributes, such as provisions regarding the protection of human rights, constraints on authorities, and judicial review (Yeh & Chang 2008; Stone Sweet 2009). Others have referred to this development and its concomitant scholarly emphasis as "global constitutionalism" (Peters 2009). Students of global constitutionalism concern themselves with understanding the tensions this characterization may instigate between states and the international community, and the implications the approach may carry for individuals seeking to make claims in regional and international legal fora. Examples of constitutionalized international regimes include the European Union, European Court of Human Rights, and World Trade Organization.

Second, perhaps the most extensive analytical effort within the field of exogenous constitutional studies has been dedicated to researching cross-national legal dialogue among judges. This phenomenon typically involves the citation of foreign or international court decisions or other external legal sources by judges in the process of deciding a court case (Choudhry 1999). This tendency has alternately been referred to as "transjudicial communication" (Slaughter 1994), "judicial globalization" (Baudenbacher 2003), "constitutional cross-fertilization" (Slaughter 2003), "transnational judicial discourse" (V.C. Jackson 2004), "transnational judicial dialogue" (Waters 2005), and "international judicial dialogue" (Krotoszynski 2006). A related concept, "constitutional borrowing," has been used to indicate everything from constitution drafters importing provisions from other constitutions in order to address similar issues (Osiatynski 2003, p.244) to judges applying ideas developed in one area of constitutional law to a different area of constitutional law (Tebbe & Tsai 2010, p.461) to even citizens looking to foreign examples when forming opinions about domestic constitutional changes (Epstein & Knight 2003, p.196). Such dialoguing or borrowing may be performed in order to: (1) identify and apply foreign constitutional logic to domestic constitutional decision-making where similar questions arise (e.g., "functionalism"); (2) understand a given state's national identity (e.g., "expressivism"); or (3) attempt to address constitutional issues using whatever external resources one might deem instructive (e.g., "bricolage") (Tushnet 1999).

Anecdotal evidence suggests that the trend occurs on a global scale—state supreme courts look to other state supreme courts, constitutional courts cite regional human rights courts, and regional tribunals cite other regional courts. On the American front, the willingness to find answers to constitutional questions from abroad appears less consistently enthusiastic. Empirical work on this subject finds that while members of the U.S. Supreme Court have referenced foreign sources of law throughout the Court's history (Calabresi & Zimdahl 2005), jurists serving on American Federal courts cite foreign courts only on rare occasions (Zaring 2006).

Third, an increasing amount of work in exogenous constitutional studies begins with the observations that the world is witnessing a rise in the number of written constitutions (Ackerman 1997) and an accompanying surge in the influence of international human rights laws (Henkin 1993; Law 2008), and proceeds to analyze the extent to which national constitutions have converged on a similar set of provisions and rights. An early, qualitative attempt to conduct a broad comparison of constitutional isomorphism finds that a majority of the independence constitutions in Africa and Asia featured provisions for religion, rights, and/or political parties that deviated from those present in the constitutional order of their former colonizers (Go 2002).

Answering the call of commentators who lamented the dearth of global, rigorous quantitative studies of comparative constitutional law (Hirschl 2005, 2006; Tushnet 2006), a handful of scholars have executed comprehensive statistical analyses testing various explanations for the apparent convergence of constitutional provisions across the world. Through an analysis of postcolonial constitutions, Go (2003) reveals that while newer constitutions tend to be more homogeneous than earlier ones, important site-specific deviations continue to persist. In particular, postcolonial constitutions exhibit signs of complexity and differentiation along with convergence. Law and Versteeg (2011) assess the claim of constitutional convergence and conclude that 90 percent of the variation in the promulgation of rights provisions can be explained in terms of two factors—comprehensiveness (e.g., how many rights are included) and ideology (e.g., the extent to which a constitution tends toward a libertarian or statist approach to rights protection). Interestingly, they observe simultaneous patterns of convergence and polarization; that is, although constitutions are becoming increasingly similar within their respective clusters (e.g., libertarian or statist), the clusters are increasingly becoming more ideologically divergent.

Gellers (2012) tests whether regional isomorphism can explain the expansion of constitutional environmental rights in three developing areas and finds that the increasing enactment of such rights within a region does not improve the likelihood that another state within the same region will follow suit. Elkins et al. (2013) show that while the prevalence of human rights in constitutions has increased over time, few fundamental guarantees enjoy near-universal adoption. However, the existence of international human rights instruments such as the Universal Declaration of Human Rights seems to have motivated the expansion of human rights in national constitutions. Goderis & Versteeg (2013) demonstrate that transnational influences affect the kinds of rights states adopt. In particular, countries are more likely to adopt rights shared by their colonial predecessor, and enacted by states with the same legal tradition, religion, colonizer, and aid donor.

In brief, much of the literature on constitutional design focuses on factors either internal or external to the state. That does not mean, however, that researchers in this area have set up a strict dichotomy. Some (e.g., Simeon 2008) have clearly acknowledged the need to examine both domestic dynamics and contextual factors present during constitutional drafting. But in terms of the present study, the motivation lies in trying to understand why constitutions in all corners of the world increasingly feature environmental rights in spite of the considerable differences among states. With this goal in mind, I argue that exogenous constitutional studies are better suited than endogenous constitutional studies to explain the expansion of constitutional environmental rights due to the presence of three supporting conditions: (1) observable constitutional convergence with respect to the inclusion of these rights; (2) the omnipresence of environmental and human rights norms during the drafting of modern constitutions; and (3) the magnitude of variation across states in terms of domestic politics, environmental performance, history, and other internal conditions.

Toward a world cultural framework of constitutional environmental rights

Thus far, I have discussed the relevance of this project to the study of IR and demonstrated how IR theory, world society theory, and constitutional design theory each lend crucial insights to the task of explaining the emergence and expansion of constitutional environmental rights. Next, I describe the gaps between the bodies of literature surveyed with respect to the topic of constitutional environmental rights. Finally, I develop a comprehensive causal story regarding the global proliferation of environmental rights by combining elements of these theories into an interdisciplinary analytical device—a world cultural framework of constitutional environmental rights.

As mentioned at the outset of this chapter, literature on constitutional environmental rights is bereft of theory. In addition, none of the theoretical enclaves reviewed here directly engages with the subject of constitutional environmental rights. While the possibility remains that this lacuna is the product of simple disinterest, I contend, rather, that this inattention has occurred due to cognizable weaknesses within each perspective. When considered in isolation, each theoretical orientation exhibits explanatory gaps that frustrate its capacity to confront the phenomenon that motivates this study. IR theory describes how and why norms change, but it does not sufficiently explain where norms and policy innovations originate. For this reason, Finnemore's (1996) point that sociological institutionalism presents a formidable challenge to political scientists continues to resonate. World society theory enumerates those hegemonic cultural concepts that configure life in the international community, but it is so macro-structural that it neglects the role of agents in promoting or changing the cultural status quo. Recent work by Meyer (2010) connecting world society theory to the individual actor has begun to atone for this shortcoming. Finally, although constitutional design theory has made significant inroads in explaining constitutional convergence, it has yet to trace specific causal mechanisms through an analysis of concrete cases or explain the variation in outcomes obtained when international and domestic norms compete or collide.

Capitalizing on the individual strengths of IR theory, world society theory, and constitutional design theory while unifying these perspectives to address flaws and fill in gaps, I propose a world cultural framework of constitutional environmental rights (see Figure 2.1).

In a world cultural framework of constitutional environmental rights, the global expansion of these legal provisions is conceptualized as an iterative process between world culture, international norms, and laws and policies propelled by an array of domestic and international actors. As illustrated in Figure 2.1, the three dominant elements of world culture—individualism, rationalization, and universalism—inhabit the macro-structure or international system that both constitutes actors and provides the script that legitimizes some norms and rejects others. Actors (mainly inter-governmental organizations) then translate these elements through international law into more concrete international norms (e.g.,

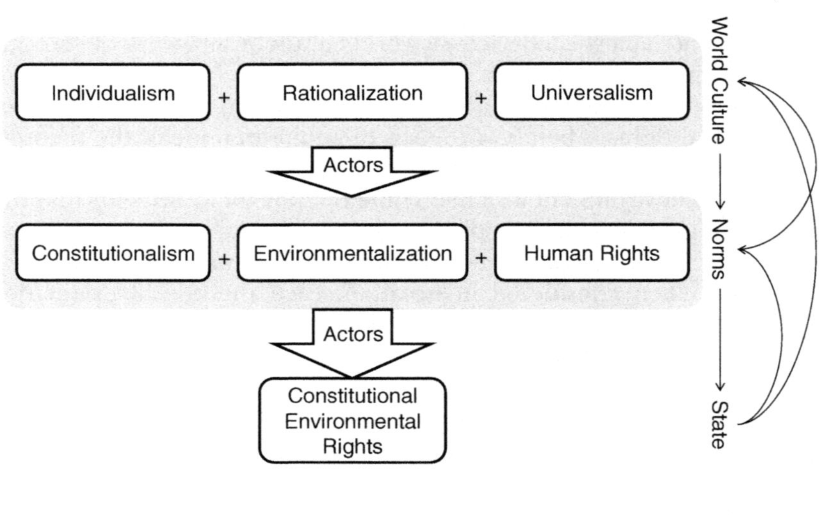

Figure 2.1 World cultural framework of constitutional environmental rights

constitutionalism, environmentalization, and human rights), which provide a bounded ideational framework that specifies the normative content deemed appropriate for uptake by political and social institutions (Risse & Sikkink 1999, p.8). This particular subset of international norms establishes the preconditions for the emergence of constitutionally instantiated human rights related to environmental protection. Finally, actors such as bureaucrats, judges, lawyers, policy-makers, and transnational activists interpret the cues given by international norms to develop or advocate for certain types of institutions, laws, and policies—in this case, constitutional environmental rights. The resulting instruments may differ slightly around the margins from one state to the next, but the overarching normative foundation that underlies the impetus to establish those instruments remains remarkably consistent. This dynamic helps to explain why some countries have entrenched environmental rights within their respective constitutions (e.g., Costa Rica), while other states "find" environmental rights hiding under existing fundamental constitutional rights (e.g., India). As the universe of institutions consolidates, problems are reframed, solved, exacerbated, or unresolved, and actors learn which laws and policies need alteration. Those actors mentioned above subsequently spring into action, producing a cycle. Thus, as long as countries adopt written constitutions, environmental concerns remain salient in popular consciousness, and the protection of human rights occupies a hegemonic position among international norms, states are likely to continue to enact constitutional environmental rights until the normative environment shifts or actors decide to change course.

The explanation above implies the existence of two important attributes of a world cultural framework of constitutional environmental rights. First, the concept incorporates a historically contingent view of international norms. While the main pillars of world culture are argued to be relatively immutable facets of modernity, the sands of time may indeed perturb the order and assortment of existing international norms, establishing a new normative environment that alters the identities of actors in the process. Therefore, this model is responsive to the changing conditions of the international arena. Second, unlike the macro-level theories of IR and world society theory, this framework helps to explain a *specific* institutional outcome—the emergence of environmental rights. I focus only on explaining the adoption of solidarity environmental rights in national constitutions, because, as mentioned in the previous chapter, other kinds of environmental rights are far less common (frustrating opportunities for quantitative analysis), alternate forms of environmental rights have slightly different aims, and placing environmental rights in a constitution affords them a special level of importance among the laws and policies of a given state.

Conclusion

Over the past four decades, constitutional environmental rights have quietly emerged to become common elements of the modern national constitution. Yet, while legal scholars have spilled much ink agonizing over their philosophical connotations and practical utility, constitutional environmental rights have evaded the attention of IR theorists altogether. As I have argued, this has been unfortunate, for constitutional environmental rights have much to teach students of IR about issues that normally monopolize scholarly debate. I have sought to bring the case of constitutional environmental rights to light and draw together literature from political science, sociology, and law to advance theory about this important worldwide development. While the result of this effort—the world cultural framework of constitutional environmental rights—provides a valuable tool for understanding this phenomenon, it serves only as a heuristic, a starting place, for the mixed methods analysis of these rights that consumes the remainder of this book.

Note

1 As a methodological caveat, it is worth recognizing that seeking to determine the role of the state where constitutional issues are concerned invites the charge of endogeneity. That is to say, the very nature of drafting a constitution represents an exercise in state sovereignty and by necessity actors aiming to influence the process focus their energies on the state, resulting in what appears to be an assertion of state primacy. However, the degree to which inputs to the constitution drafting process originate from within the state vary considerably, representing a range of possibilities along a spectrum from the purely autochthonous to the externally imposed and every shade in between. Therefore, in light of the cases and the presence of endogeneity, I tentatively conclude that with respect to constitutional environmental rights, although relevant norms and actors involved emanate from the international community, the state remains the primary site of norm contestation and the desired level of governance for addressing the nexus between ecological protection and human rights.

Bibliography

Acemoglu, D. & Robinson, J.A., 2000. Why Did the West Extend the Franchise? Democracy, Inequality, and Growth in Historical Perspective. *The Quarterly Journal of Economics*, 115(4), pp.1167–1199.

Acharya, A., 2004. How Ideas Spread: Whose Norms Matter? Norm Localization and Institutional Change in Asian Regionalism. *International Organization*, 58(2), pp.239–275.

Ackerman, B., 1997. The Rise of World Constitutionalism. *Virginia Law Review*, 83, pp.771–797.

Andonova, L.B. & Mitchell, R.B., 2010. The Rescaling of Global Environmental Politics. *Annual Review of Environment and Resources*, 35(1), pp.255–282.

Arato, A., 1995. Forms of Constitution Making and Theories of Democracy. *Cardozo Law Review*, 17, pp.191–231.

Arjomand, S.A., 2000. International Sociology into the New Millennium: The Global Sociological Community and the Challenge to the Periphery. *International Sociology*, 15(1), pp.5–10.

Axelrod, R. & Keohane, R.O., 1985. Achieving Cooperation Under Anarchy: Strategies and Institutions. *World Politics*, 38(1), pp.226–254.

Barkin, J.S., 2003. Realist Constructivism. *International Studies Review*, 5(3), pp.325–342.

Baudenbacher, C., 2003. Judicial Globalization: New Development or Old Wine in New Bottles? *Texas International Law Journal*, 38(3), pp.505–526.

Berger, G., Flynn, A., Hines, F., & Johns, R., 2001. Ecological Modernization as a Basis for Environmental Policy: Current Environmental Discourse and Policy and the Implications on Environmental Supply Chain Management. *Innovation: The European Journal of Social Science Research*, 14(1), pp.55–72.

Betsill, M.M. & Corell, E., 2001. NGO Influence in International Environmental Negotiations: A Framework for Analysis. *Global Environmental Politics*, 1(4), pp.65–85.

Björkdahl, A., 2002. Norms in International Relations: Some Conceptual and Methodological Reflections. *Cambridge Review of International Affairs*, 15(1), pp.9–23.

Boli, J., 1987. Human Rights or State Expansion? Cross-National Definitions of Constitutional Rights, 1870–1970. In *Institutional Structure: Constituting State, Society, and the Individual.* Newbury Park: SAGE, pp.133–149.

Boli, J., 1999. Conclusion: World Authority Structures and Legitimations. In J. Boli & G.M. Thomas, eds. *Constructing World Culture: International Nongovernmental Organizations Since 1875.* Stanford: Stanford University Press, pp.267–300.

Boli, J. & Thomas, G.M., 1997. World Culture in the World Polity: A Century of International Non-Governmental Organization. *American Sociological Review*, 62(2), pp.171–190.

Boli, J. & Thomas, G.M., 1999. INGOs and the Organization of World Culture. In J. Boli & G.M. Thomas, eds. *Constructing World Culture: International Nongovernmental Organizations Since 1875.* Stanford: Stanford University Press, pp.13–49.

Boyd, D.R., 2012. *The Environmental Rights Revolution: A Global Study of Constitutions, Human Rights, and the Environment*, Vancouver, BC: UBC Press.

Boyle, E.H., McMorris, B.J. & Gomez, M., 2002. Local Conformity to International Norms: The Case of Female Genital Cutting. *International Sociology*, 17(1), pp.5–33.

Brown, C., 2001. World Society and the English School: An "International Society" Perspective on World Society. *European Journal of International Relations*, 7(4), pp.423–441.

Brown, N.J., 2008. Reason, Interest, Rationality, and Passion in Constitution Drafting. *Perspectives on Politics*, 6(4), pp.675–689.

Buchanan, J.M. & Tullock, G., 1962. *The Calculus of Consent: Logical Foundations of Constitutional Democracy*, Ann Arbor: University of Michigan Press.

Bull, H., 1977. *The Anarchical Society: A Study of Order in World Politics*, New York: Columbia University Press.

Bull, H. & Watson, A., 1984. *The Expansion of International Society*, Oxford: Clarendon Press.

Busch, P.-O., Gupta, A. & Falkner, R., 2012. International-Domestic Linkages and Policy Convergence. In F. Biermann & P. Pattberg, eds. *Global Environmental Governance Reconsidered.* Cambridge: MIT Press, pp.199–218.

Buttel, F.H., 2000. Ecological Modernization as Social Theory. *Geoforum*, 31(1), pp.57–65.

Buzan, B., 1993. From International System to International Society: Structural Realism and Regime Theory Meet the English School. *International Organization*, 47(3), pp.327–352.

Calabresi, S. & Zimdahl, S., 2005. The Supreme Court and Foreign Sources of Law: Two Hundred Years of Practice and the Juvenile Death Penalty Decision. *William and Mary Law Review*, 47(3), pp.743–909.

Checkel, J., 1997. International Norms and Domestic Politics: Bridging the Rationalist–Constructivist Divide. *European Journal of International Relations*, 3(4), pp.473–495.

Checkel, J., 1998. The Constructivist Turn in International Relations Theory. *World Politics*, 50(2), pp.324–348.

Checkel, J., 1999. Norms, Institutions, and National Identity in Contemporary Europe. *International Studies Quarterly*, 43(1), pp.83–114.

Choudhry, S., 1999. Globalization in Search of Justification: Toward a Theory of Comparative Constitutional Interpretation. *Indiana Law Journal*, 74, pp.819–948.

Clark, I., 1999. *Globalization and International Relations Theory*, Oxford: Oxford University Press.

Compagnon, D., Chan, S. & Mert, A., 2012. The Changing Role of the State. In F. Biermann & P. Pattberg, eds. *Global Environmental Governance Reconsidered.* Cambridge: MIT Press, pp.237–263.

Conca, K., 2015. *An Unfinished Foundation: The United Nations and Global Environmental Governance*, New York: Oxford University Press.

Cortell, A.P. & Davis, J.W., 2000. Understanding the Domestic Impact of International Norms: A Research Agenda. *International Studies Review*, 2(1), pp.65–87.

DiMaggio, P.J. & Powell, W.W., 1991. The Iron Cage Revisited: Institutionalized Isomorphism and Collective Rationality in Organizational Fields. In W.W. Powell & P.J. DiMaggio, eds. *The New Institutionalism in Organizational Analysis.* Chicago: University of Chicago Press, pp.63–82.

Drezner, D.W., 2001. Globalization and Policy Convergence. *International Studies Review*, 3(1), pp.53–78.

Dryzek, J.S., 2013. *The Politics of the Earth: Environmental Discourses*, 3rd ed., Oxford: Oxford University Press.

Elkins, Z., Ginsburg, T. & Simmons, B., 2013. Getting to Rights: Treaty Ratification, Constitutional Convergence, and Human Rights Practice. *Harvard International Law Journal*, 54(1), pp.61–95.

Elliott, M.A., 2007. Human Rights and the Triumph of the Individual in World Culture. *Cultural Sociology*, 1(3), pp.343–363.

Elster, J., 1995. Forces and Mechanisms in the Constitution-Making Process. *Duke Law Journal*, 45(2), pp.364–396.

Epstein, L. & Knight, J., 2003. Epstein and Knight: Constitutional Borrowing and Nonborrowing. *International Journal of Constitutional Law*, 1(2), pp.196–223.

Falkner, R., 2012. Global Environmentalism and the Greening of International Society. *International Affairs*, 88(3), pp.503–522.

Fearon, J. & Wendt, A., 2002. Rationalism v. Constructivism: A Skeptical View. In W. Carlsnaes, T. Risse, & B.A. Simmons, eds. *Handbook of International Relations*. London: SAGE, pp.52–72.

Finnemore, M., 1996. Norms, Culture, and World Politics: Insights from Sociology's Institutionalism. *International Organization*, 50(2), pp.325–347.

Finnemore, M. & Sikkink, K., 1998. International Norm Dynamics and Political Change. *International Organization*, 52(4), pp.887–917.

Florini, A., 1996. The Evolution of International Norms. *International Studies Quarterly*, 40(3), pp.363–389.

Frank, D.J., 1997. Science, Nature, and the Globalization of the Environment, 1870–1990. *Social Forces*, 76(2), pp.409–437.

Frank, D.J., Hironaka, A. & Schofer, E., 2000. The Nation-State and the Natural Environment over the Twentieth Century. *American Sociological Review*, 65, pp.96–116.

Frank, D.J., Longhofer, W. & Schofer, E., 2007. World Society, NGOs, and Environmental Policy Reform in Asia. *International Journal of Comparative Sociology*, 48(4), pp.275–295.

Gellers, J.C., 2012. Greening Constitutions with Environmental Rights: Testing the Isomorphism Thesis. *Review of Policy Research*, 29(4), pp.523–543.

Go, J., 2002. Modeling the State: Postcolonial Constitutions in Asia and Africa. *Southeast Asian Studies*, 39(4), pp.558–583.

Go, J., 2003. A Globalizing Constitutionalism? Views from the Postcolony, 1945–2000. *International Sociology*, 18(1), pp.71–95.

Goderis, B. & Versteeg, M., 2013. Transnational Constitutions. *Social Science Research Network*. Available at: http://papers.ssrn.com/abstract=2216582 [Accessed December 14, 2013].

Goodman, R. & Jinks, D., 2004. How to Influence States: Socialization and International Human Rights Law. *Duke Law Journal*, 54(3), pp.621–703.

Gough, C. & Shackley, S., 2001. The Respectable Politics of Climate Change: The Epistemic Communities and NGOs. *International Affairs*, 77(2), pp.329–346.

Gourevitch, P., 1978. The Second Image Reversed: The International Sources of Domestic Politics. *International Organization*, 32(4), pp.881–912.

Gurowitz, A., 1999. Mobilizing International Norms: Domestic Actors, Immigrants, and the Japanese State. *World Politics*, 51(3), pp.413–445.

Hafner-Burton, E.M., 2008. Sticks and Stones: Naming and Shaming the Human Rights Enforcement Problem. *International Organization*, 62, pp.689–716.

Hafner-Burton, E.M. & Tsutsui, K., 2005. Human Rights in a Globalizing World: The Paradox of Empty Promises. *American Journal of Sociology*, 110(5), pp.1373–1411.

Halliday, T.C., 2009. Recursivity of Global Normmaking: A Sociolegal Agenda. *Annual Review of Law and Social Science*, 5(1), pp.263–289.

Hallstrom, L.K., 2004. Eurocratising Enlargement? EU Elites and NGO Participation in European Environmental Policy. *Environmental Politics*, 13(1), pp.175–193.

Hayo, B. & Voigt, S., 2010. Determinants of Constitutional Change: Why do Countries Change their Form of Government? *Journal of Comparative Economics*, 38(3), pp.283–305.

Henkin, L., 1993. A New Birth of Constitutionalism: Genetic Influences and Genetic Defects. *Cardozo Law Review*, 14, pp.533–548.

Hironaka, A., 2002. The Globalization of Environmental Protection: The Case of Environmental Impact Assessment. *International Journal of Comparative Sociology*, 43(1), pp.65–78.

Hirschl, R., 2005. The Question of Case Selection in Comparative Constitutional Law. *American Journal of Comparative Law*, 53(1), pp.125–155.

Hirschl, R., 2006. On the Blurred Methodological Matrix of Comparative Constitutional Law. In S. Choudhry, ed. *The Migration of Constitutional Ideas*. New York: Cambridge University Press, pp.39–66. Available at: http://dx.doi.org/10.1017/CBO9780511493683.002 [Accessed October 1, 2016].

Ho, P., 2001. Greening Without Conflict? Environmentalism, NGOs and Civil Society in China. *Development and Change*, 32(5), pp.893–921.

Howard, A.E.D., 2009. A Traveler from an Antique Land: The Modern Renaissance of Comparative Constitutionalism. *Virginia Journal of International Law*, 50(1), pp.3–41.

Ikenberry, G.J. & Kupchan, C.A., 1990. Socialization and Hegemonic Power. *International Organization*, 44(3), pp.283–315.

Jackson, P.T., 2004. Bridging the Gap: Toward a Realist-Constructivist Dialogue. *International Studies Review*, 6(2), pp.337–352.

Jackson, V.C., 2004. Constitutional Dialogue and Human Dignity: States and Transnational Constitutional Discourse. *Montana Law Review*, 65, pp.15–40.

Jorgenson, A.K., Dick, C. & Shandra, J.M., 2011. World Economy, World Society, and Environmental Harms in Less-Developed Countries. *Sociological Inquiry*, 81(1), pp.53–87.

Kamieniecki, S. & Granzeier, M.S., 1998. Eco-Cultural Security and Indigenous Self-Determination: Moving Toward a New Conception of Sovereignty. In K. Litfin, ed. *The Greening of Sovereignty in World Politics*. Cambridge: MIT Press, pp.257–274.

Katzenstein, P.J., Keohane, R.O. & Krasner, S.D., 1998. International Organization and the Study of World Politics. *International Organization*, 52(4), pp.645–685.

Kaufmann, C.D. & Pape, R.A., 1999. Explaining Costly International Moral Action: Britain's Sixty-Year Campaign against the Atlantic Slave Trade. *International Organization*, 53(4), pp.631–668.

Keck, M.E. & Sikkink, K., 1999. Transnational Advocacy Networks in International and Regional Politics. *International Social Science Journal*, 51(159), pp.89–101.

Keith, L.C., 2002. Constitutional Provisions for Individual Human Rights (1977–1996): Are They More than Mere "Window Dressing?" *Political Research Quarterly*, 55(1), pp.111–143.

Keohane, R.O., 1984. *After Hegemony: Cooperation and Discord in the World Political Economy*, Princeton: Princeton University Press.

Kerr, C., 1983. *The Future of Industrial Societies: Convergence or Continuing Diversity?*, Cambridge: Harvard University Press.

Klotz, A.J., 1995. *Norms in International Relations: The Struggle against Apartheid*, Ithaca, NY: Cornell University Press.

Koremenos, B., Lipson, C. & Snidal, D., 2001. The Rational Design of International Institutions. *International Organization*, 55(4), pp.761–799.

Krotoszynski, R.J.J., 2006. I'd Like to Teach the World to Sing (in Perfect

Harmony): International Judicial Dialogue and the Muses: Reflections of the Perils and the Promise of International Judicial Dialogue. *Michigan Law Review*, 104(6), pp.1321–1359.

Kuehls, T., 1998. Between Sovereignty and Environment: An Exploration of the Discourse of Government. In K. Litfin, ed. *The Greening of Sovereignty in World Politics*. Cambridge: MIT Press, pp.31–53.

Law, D.S., 2008. Globalization and the Future of Constitutional Rights. *Northwestern University Law Review*, 102(3), pp.1–89.

Law, D.S. & Versteeg, M., 2011. The Evolution and Ideology of Global Constitutionalism. *California Law Review*, 99, pp.1163–1254.

Lechner, F.J., 1991. The Case Against Secularization: A Rebuttal. *Social Forces*, 69(4), pp.1103–1119.

Legro, J.W., 1997. Which Norms Matter? Revisiting the "Failure" of Internationalism. *International Organization*, 51(1), pp.31–63.

Lijphart, A., 1991. Constitutional Choices for New Democracies. *Journal of Democracy*, 2(1), pp.72–84.

Litfin, K., 1998. The Greening of Sovereignty: An Introduction. In K. Litfin, ed. *The Greening of Sovereignty in World Politics*. Cambridge: MIT Press, pp.1–27.

Mearsheimer, J.J., 1994. The False Promise of International Institutions. *International Security*, 19(3), pp.5–49.

Meyer, J.W., 1987. The World Polity and the Authority of the Nation-State. In G.M. Thomas, J.W. Meyer, F.O. Ramirez, & J. Boli, eds. *Institutional Structure: Constituting State, Society, and the Individual*. Newbury Park: SAGE, pp.41–70.

Meyer, J.W., 2010. World Society, Institutional Theories, and the Actor. *Annual Review of Sociology*, 36(1), pp.1–20.

Meyer, J.W., Boli, J. & Thomas, G.M., 1987. Ontology and Rationalization in the Western Cultural Account. In G.M. Thomas, J.W. Meyer, F.O. Ramirez, & J. Boli, eds. *Institutional Structure: Constituting State, Society, and the Individual*. Newbury Park: SAGE, pp.12–37.

Meyer, J.W., Boli, J., Thomas, G.M., & Ramirez, F.O., 1997. World Society and the Nation–State. *American Journal of Sociology*, 103(1), pp.144–181.

Mol, A.P.J., 1997. Ecological Modernization: Industrial Transformations and Environmental Reform. In M.R. Redclift & G. Woodgate, eds. *The International Handbook of Environmental Sociology*. London: Edward Elgar, pp.138–149.

Mol, A.P.J., 2002. Ecological Modernization and the Global Economy. *Global Environmental Politics*, 2(2), pp.92–115.

Nadelmann, E.A., 1990. Global Prohibition Regimes: The Evolution of Norms in International Society. *International Organization*, 44(4), pp.479–526.

Neuman, G.L., 2003. Human Rights and Constitutional Rights: Harmony and Dissonance. *Stanford Law Review*, 55, pp.1863–1900.

Osiatynski, W., 2003. Paradoxes of Constitutional Borrowing. *International Journal of Constitutional Law*, 1(2), pp.244–268.

Oye, K.A., 1985. Explaining Cooperation Under Anarchy: Hypotheses and Strategies. *World Politics*, 38(1), pp.1–24.

Peters, A., 2009. The Merits of Global Constitutionalism. *Indiana Journal of Global Legal Studies*, 16(2), pp.397–411.

Raustiala, K., 1997. States, NGOs, and International Environmental Institutions. *International Studies Quarterly*, 41(4), pp.719–740.

Raymond, G.A., 1997. Problems and Prospects in the Study of International Norms. *Mershon International Studies Review*, 41(2), pp.205–245.

Risse, T. & Sikkink, K., 1999. The Socialization of International Human Rights Norms into Domestic Practices: Introduction. In T. Risse, S.C. Ropp, & K. Sikkink, eds. *The Power of Human Rights: International Norms and Domestic Change*. Cambridge: Cambridge University Press, pp.1–38.

Sandholtz, W., 2007. *Prohibiting Plunder : How Norms Change*, New York: Oxford University Press.

Sandholtz, W., 2008. Dynamics of International Norm Change: Rules Against Wartime Plunder. *European Journal of International Relations*, 14(1), pp.101–131.

Saunders, C., 2014. The Impact of Internationalisation on National Constitutions. In A. Chen, ed. *Constitutionalism in Asia in the Early Twenty-First Century*. Cambridge: Cambridge University Press.

Schofer, E. & Hironaka, A., 2005. The Effects of World Society on Environmental Protection Outcomes. *Social Forces*, 84(1), pp.25–47.

Schofer, E., Hironaka, A., John, D., & Longhofer, W., 2012. Sociological Institutionalism and World Society. In E. Amenta, K. Nash, & A. Scott, eds. *The Wiley-Blackwell Companion to Political Sociology*. Oxford: Blackwell, pp.57–68.

Shandra, J.M., Shor, E. & London, B., 2009. World Polity, Unequal Ecological Exchange, and Organic Water Pollution: A Cross-National Analysis of Developing Nations. *Human Ecology Review*, 16(1), pp.53–63.

Simeon, R., 2008. Constitutional Design and Change in Federal Systems: Issues and Questions. *Publius: The Journal of Federalism*, 39(2), pp.241–261.

Slaughter, A.-M., 1994. A Typology of Transjudicial Communication. *University of Richmond Law Review*, 29, pp.99–138.

Slaughter, A.-M., 2003. A Global Community of Courts. *Harvard International Law Journal*, 44(1), pp.191–220.

Spaargaren, G. & Mol, A.P.J., 1992. Sociology, Environment and Modernity: Ecological Modernization as a Theory of Social Change. *Society and Natural Resources*, 5(4), pp.323–344.

Stone Sweet, A., 2009. Constitutionalism, Legal Pluralism, and International Regimes. *Indiana Journal of Global Legal Studies*, 16(2), pp.621–645.

Tebbe, N. & Tsai, R.L., 2010. Constitutional Borrowing. *Michigan Law Review*, 108, pp.459–522.

Ticchi, D. & Vindigni, A., 2010. Endogenous Constitutions. *Economic Journal*, 120(543), pp.1–39.

Tushnet, M., 1999. The Possibilities of Comparative Constitutional Law. *Yale Law Journal*, 108(6), pp.1225–1309.

Tushnet, M., 2006. Some Reflections on Method in Comparative Constitutional Law. In S. Choudhry, ed. *The Migration of Constitutional Ideas*. New York: Cambridge University Press, pp.67–83. Available at: http://dx.doi.org/10.1017/CBO9780511493683.003 [Accessed October 1, 2016].

Vasi, I.B., 2007. Thinking Globally, Planning Nationally and Acting Locally: Nested Organizational Fields and the Adoption of Environmental Practices. *Social Forces*, 86(1), pp.113–135.

Walt, S.M., 1998. International Relations: One World, Many Theories. *Foreign Policy*, (110), pp.29–46.

Wapner, P., 1995. Politics Beyond the State: Environmental Activism and World

Civic Politics. *World Politics*, 47(3), pp.311–340.

Wapner, P., 1998. Reorienting State Sovereignty: Rights and Responsibilities in the Environmental Age. In K. Litfin, ed. *The Greening of Sovereignty in World Politics*. Cambridge: MIT Press, pp.275–297.

Waters, M.A., 2005. Mediating Norms and Identity: The Role of Transnational Judicial Dialogue in Creating and Enforcing International Law. *Georgetown Law Journal*, 93, pp.487–574.

Weinrib, L.E., 2006. The Postwar Paradigm and American Exceptionalism. In S. Choudhry, ed. *The Migration of Constitutional Ideas*. New York: Cambridge University Press, pp.84–111.

Wendt, A., 1992. Anarchy is what States Make of it: The Social Construction of Power Politics. *International Organization*, 46(2), pp.391–425.

Wendt, A., 1995. Constructing International Politics. *International Security*, 20(1), pp.71–81.

Yearly, S., 1996. *Sociology, Environmentalism, Globalization: Reinventing the Globe*, London: SAGE.

Yeh, J.-R. & Chang, W.-C., 2008. The Emergence of Transnational Constitutionalism: Its Features, Challenges and Solutions. *Penn State International Law Review*, 27(1), pp.89–124.

Zaring, D., 2006. The Use of Foreign Decisions by Federal Courts: An Empirical Analysis. *Journal of Empirical Legal Studies*, 3(2), pp.297–331.

Zürn, M., 1998. The Rise of International Environmental Politics: A Review of Current Research. *World Politics*, 50(4), pp.617–649.

Chapter 3

The global expansion of environmental rights

Introduction

Chapter 1 recounted the historical origins of environmental rights and characterized their expression within national constitutions throughout the world. Chapter 2 erected an interdisciplinary theoretical framework designed to explain this phenomenon. The next step is to apply this framework and test competing explanations for the global expansion of environmental rights using social science methods. Following Lieberman's (2005) suggestion, I employ an integrated approach known as "nested analysis" that harnesses the strengths of both quantitative analysis and in-depth case studies as a means of improving the likelihood of obtaining valid causal inferences. Among its many benefits, nested analysis can help researchers identify potential case studies using the results of statistical analyses, focus the efforts of comparisons, and assess the real world reliability of observed statistical relationships (Lieberman 2005, p.435). This analytical strategy manifests in the present study through the use of a large-N statistical analysis (this chapter) that informs the selection of two cases that I subject to further scrutiny (the next chapter).

In this chapter I embark on the first stage of this dual-pronged process by testing three theoretical explanations for the proliferation of constitutional environmental rights using survival analysis, a kind of statistical technique useful for assessing how different factors affect the time until an event occurs (in this case, the adoption of a constitutional environmental right). I argue that a theory based on norm socialization offers more explanatory purchase than theories focused on domestic politics or rationalist–materialist considerations. The chapter begins with an examination of current and alternative explanations for the spread of constitutional environmental rights and proceeds with a discussion of the results from a theoretically informed global quantitative analysis.

Current explanations

Scholars have offered many potential explanations for the trend toward constitutionalization of environmental rights that began in the 1970s. Initial efforts were largely descriptive and anecdotal. Some hypotheses speak to conditions specific to certain regions. Consider the post-communist states of Eastern Europe. Following the demise of communism in 1989, leaders of these states sought to strengthen domestic human rights instruments because of "the lack of protection of basic rights during the communist era" (Henckaerts & Van der Jeught 1998, p.476). More specifically, the enactment of environmental rights in post-communist constitutions may have been influenced by the desire to elevate the level of progressive ideology contained within these charters and compensate citizens for past environmental harms. Some have argued that post-communist states placed environmental rights in their constitutions because the old constitutions included environmental social rights, and policy-makers felt that the new democratic constitutions "must not pale in comparison" (Brandl & Bungert 1992, p.99). Another observer adds that post-communist states included "comparatively bold environmental rights" in their constitutions "perhaps to spearhead the cleanup of a half-century of neglect" (Gravelle 1997, p.633). These rationales appear attractive considering that "[a]ll constitutions contain some elements of a polemic against the immediate past" (Duchacek 1968, p.94).

Other hypotheses refer more generally to the pursuit of legitimacy in the eyes of the international community.[1] For example, Brazil's adoption of a suite of environmental statutes, establishment of a new environmental ministry, and promulgation of "the right to an ecologically balanced environment" in the 1988 Constitution have been speculatively regarded as part of a larger effort "to gain international legitimacy and credibility" (Fernandes 1996, p.279).

Some researchers suggest that the global expansion of environmental rights represents a logical outgrowth of the increased international concern about the state of the environment beginning in the 1960s (Shelton 1991; Bándi 1992; Popović 1996). However, legal scholars writing on this issue have generally accepted this explanation without delving further into the reasons why so many countries incorporated this constitutional innovation over such a (relatively) short period of time. To be sure, states likely did not exhibit the same degree of concern for the environment such that entrenching environmental rights in national constitutions was deemed necessary in most cases. Nor did states universally possess the financial, human, and technological resources necessary to fully implement such provisions. So what explains the fairly rapid and geographically diverse uptake of environmental rights? As I contended at the beginning of this book, the environmental concern argument insufficiently addresses the fact that constitutional convergence on environmental rights occurred against a backdrop of important national differences.

Since these early attempts to explain the emergence of constitutional environmental rights, several scholars have sought to analyze this development using more sophisticated techniques. Hancock (2003) seeks to address this puzzle using a global survey. He finds that the growing recognition of environmental rights in state constitutions relates to the international normative environment and social movement activism. However, the author is careful to point out that the results of the survey are likely not generalizable due to the low response rate (only three subjects replied). In addition, two of the three respondents represented countries that have adopted constitutional environmental rights—Argentina (in 1994) and Georgia (in 2003). These positive cases say little about why certain states did *not* adopt such rights. As Boyd (2012, pp.51–52) points out, since the 1970s, at least 40 countries have made changes to their constitution that did not include environmental rights or responsibilities.

Gutmann et al. (2013) present an international, quantitative examination of the expansion of constitutional environmental rights. Their study tests various explanations for environmental constitutionalism, which the authors arrange into four groups of potential determinants— economic factors, environmental factors, institutional factors, and preferences. The proposed determinants mainly concern factors endogenous to the state that might influence constitutional changes or environmental attitudes. Using survival analysis on unbalanced panel data, the team of German law and economics scholars finds that the adoption of constitutional environmental rights is significantly associated with "the level of democracy, legal tradition, sustainability of tourism, and major changes to the constitution" as well as spatial diffusion (Gutmann et al. 2013, p.3). Ultimately, this work approaches the research question that motivates the present study mainly through the lens of endogenous constitutional studies, but does not fully explore the potential explanatory value of exogenous and normative factors.

Boyd (2012) paints a response to the question regarding why countries have increasingly sought to entrench environmental rights in their respective constitutions using broad strokes. He describes the rise of constitutional environmental rights as a product of three major international trends—the move toward constitutional democracy (mainly among developing nations), a global "rights revolution" (Epp 1998), and the global environmental crisis. In terms of constitutional democracy, countries seeking to recover from fascist, colonial, and communist rule authored new constitutions that included contemporary human rights. Regarding the rights revolution, recognition and protection of human rights expanded greatly following the end of World War II, along with the idea that in order for rights to be meaningful they should be formally codified in law. Finally, on the importance of the global environmental crisis, the author maintains that "widespread public awareness of global environmental problems emerged in the 1960s," which helps to explain why "the right to a healthy environmental is not found in pioneering human rights instruments such as the *Universal Declaration of Human Rights* (1948), the *International Covenant on Civil and Political Rights* (1966), or the *International Covenant on Economic, Social, and Cultural Rights* (1966)" (Boyd 2012, pp.9–10, 12).

The foregoing discussion of global trends offers a mainly historical account of the relationship between the development of constitutional environmental rights and the larger international normative environment. However, like Gutmann et al., Boyd does not examine the explanatory possibilities contained within IR theory. In addition, like Hancock, Boyd presents a conclusion that is not based on a systematic empirical analysis designed specifically to analyze why certain countries adopt constitutional environmental rights while others do not. Finally, the three trends identified are primarily global in scope, thus overlooking the role of domestic factors in encouraging the spread of environmental rights. This book seeks to correct for the various deficits in the literature reviewed above by systematically assessing the emergence of constitutional environmental rights from the vantage point of macro-level theories (e.g., IR theory and world society theory), along with explanations focused on factors internal to the state.

Alternative explanations

As detailed in the previous section, the three major empirical studies on constitutional environmental rights (Hancock 2003; Boyd 2012; Gutmann et al. 2013) all lack a theoretical explanation for the trend observed. Therefore, in this section I develop three theoretically informed alternative explanations for the widespread adoption of constitutional environmental rights.

First, a theory of norm socialization, based on world society theory and a constructivist approach to IR, might explain why certain states adopt environmental rights and others do not. On this question, world society theory (Meyer et al. 1997a) is instructive and accords with the constructivist approach to IR. While states may act and be reconstructed in response to the behavior of actors such as other states, transnational activists, and intergovernmental organizations, this redefinition is more the result of being situated within a broader world culture than it is a reflection of internal rational calculations regarding the pursuit of self-interest. Therefore, world society theorists and constructivists might speculate that a country would be socialized through interactions in international society to adopt environmental rights as a "symbol of national identity and democratic commitment" (Ackerman 1997, p.783).

Political scientists and sociologists alike identify transnational activists and the networks through which they operate as agents who engage in socialization, spreading progressive ideas and norms throughout the international community and deploying them in local contexts (Keck & Sikkink 1998; Price 1998; Boli 1999; Boli & Thomas 1999; Risse & Sikkink 1999; Tarrow 2001). In the environmental domain, TANs may play a central role in raising consciousness about environmental injustice within a state, and promoting institutional changes to address environmental problems (Wapner 1995). Thus, in a theory of norm socialization, borderless advocacy groups leverage resources that would otherwise be unavailable to domestic groups, compelling states to pursue the constitutional enactment of environmental rights.

Second, a rationalist–materialist account of IR may provide an explanation for the phenomenon of interest. World powers might coerce weaker states to adopt new norms by "manipulating material incentives" or "altering the *substantive beliefs* of leaders in other nations" (Ikenberry & Kupchan 1990, p.285; emphasis in original). To be sure, powerful states have indeed influenced the design of national constitutions, a non-trivial number of which have been "drafted and adopted in the shadow of the gun" (Feldman 2005, p.858). Throughout history, "dominant states have been known to impose a constitutional template on weaker states or to demand conformity to such a template as a condition of normal relations" (Law & Versteeg 2011, p.1178). Therefore, rationalists might argue that states adopt constitutional environmental rights as a result of coercion or pressure by a hegemon (e.g., a global or regional power).

Another rationalist–materialist explanation for the phenomenon might be that a state wishes to send a signal to potential investors about the strength of the rule of law in the country and its commitment to human rights in order to secure foreign direct investment (FDI). In broad terms, rights represent costly commitments made by states that ideally place the interests of citizens above those of the government. The enactment of rights suggests a government's willingness to relinquish some authority in the short term in order to secure societal benefits in the long term. Investors interpret this action to mean that the government is unlikely to "pose a threat of expropriation" (Farber 2002, p.83), thus reducing the risk of investing in the state. Moving from promulgation to implementation, observable adherence to human rights conveys stability and transparency, signs that a state offers a hospitable environment for foreign capital (Law 2008, p.50).

Previous work in this area shows that foreign investors do reward states that seek to protect rights (Blanton & Blanton 2006; Busse & Hefeker 2007). The causal arrow may also point in the opposite direction, however. Empirical research demonstrates that government respect for physical integrity rights and political rights and civil liberties increases as the level of FDI in a country grows (Richards et al. 2001, p.219). A related but opposite argument, that firms looking to invest abroad flock to so-called "pollution havens" where environmental regulations are weak or nonexistent, is generally not supported by the literature (e.g., Zarsky 1999, p.47; Mol 2002, p.104; Petrović-Randjelović 2007, p.188).

States may enact certain provisions to appease donor countries seeking to offer financial support to countries that take measures to promote the protection of human rights or the environment. For example, previous work has shown that the distribution of U.S. foreign aid is positively associated with a recipient country's efforts to safeguard human rights (Abrams & Lewis 1993, p.819). Constitutions offer donors highly visible cues regarding the extent to which states take human rights seriously, so "when aid is conditional upon human rights, aid recipients face financial incentives to constitutionally commit to rights" (Goderis & Versteeg 2013, p.4). In addition, weaker states may signal their commitment to protecting nature by signing environmental treaties in the hopes of "attracting more Western funding through a kind of permanent if implicit bargaining" (Compagnon et al. 2012, p.240). Even in situations in which states face a diminishing capability to address environmental problems, "governments use the conservation of the environment as a bargaining chip with donor countries to obtain economic gains" (Compagnon et al. 2012, p.252). In the present study, environmental rights, which are often classified as third-generation human rights, may be viewed as elements of the broader human rights initiative and environmental law portfolio undertaken by a country to solicit support in the form of aid or investment. Therefore, under a rationalist–materialist perspective states might adopt environmental rights to satisfy the demands of a hegemon, fall in line with other countries in the region in order to avoid appearing like a laggard and losing a competitive edge in attracting investment, or pursue self-interested goals such as increasing foreign assistance.

Third, a theory focused on domestic politics may assist in answering the main research question. At the state level, environmental policy innovations may come about as a response to public opinion on environmental issues (Calvert 1979), efforts of domestic social movement organizations (Rucht 1999, p.215), policy entrepreneurship (Meijerink & Huitema 2010), and political leadership (Steinberg 2001, p.81), or a combination of internal factors (Agnone 2007). More specifically, the pressure to adopt environmental rights may come from a range of actors within a state who seek to right historic wrongs (Henckaerts & Van der Jeught 1998, p.476) or spur environmental cleanup efforts (Gravelle 1997, p.633). These actors may utilize a variety of tactics, such as protests, letter writing campaigns, lobbying, litigation, or voting to encourage domestic leaders to address the issue of environmental justice through the enactment of environmental rights.

It is important to note that a comprehensive and realistic explanation for the expansion of constitutional environmental rights may involve overlapping theories. For instance, norm socialization may function simultaneously with rationalist–materialist considerations like power and wealth (Simmons 2000); TANs may provide resources to assist domestic pressure groups (Keck & Sikkink 1999, p.89); domestic interest groups may operate under rationalist–materialist logics (Olson 1965); and international norms may be invoked by domestic groups (Cardenas 2004, p.215). The growing incidence of constitutional environmental rights, like environmentalism in general, "is most likely a complex social phenomenon, a mixture of social perceptions, local histories and environmental realities, international relationships and influences, and unique cultural and structural features of particular countries and regions" (Brechin 1999, p.807). Therefore, the possibility looms that the most robust explanation for the observed trend might be complex and multi-level.

Before discussing the reasons why norm socialization presents the most defensible option among the theories reviewed, I address the viability of two potential rationalist–materialist explanations for the emergence of constitutional environmental rights—functionalism and hegemonic coercion. In general, applying a functionalist logic to the design of institutions ignores three important limitations: (1) institutional designers may act according to what they deem is an appropriate course of action in a given setting and situation rather than by considering what actions would be most effective; (2) actors may have short time horizons that are incommensurable with the long-term objectives institutions are established to achieve; and (3) designing institutions may produce unanticipated consequences given the complexity of modern social organization (Pierson 2000, pp.478–486). In terms of constitutional environmental rights, these drawbacks suggest that (1) such rights may be adopted for reasons related to forging a national identity or placating domestic concerns about environmental quality irrespective of their potential efficacy; (2) politicians seeking reelection might have little to gain by adopting rights or environmental policies whose impacts might not be realized over the term of their time in public office (Underdal 2010); and (3) the fact that several kinds of actors are involved in most constitution drafting processes (Ginsburg et al. 2009) and there exist many potential veto points along the way to ratification diminishes the likelihood that a substantial number of countries throughout the world enact rights featuring remarkably similar phrasing for reasons that are specific to that particular state alone.

Some might argue that the trend toward constitutional recognition of environmental rights reflects a practical and unsurprising response to domestic environmental degradation. Recognizing the existence of environmental problems, the argument goes, states will be naturally inclined to enact constitutional environmental rights as a means of fixing those problems. However, this functionalist reasoning does not withstand the test of empirical scrutiny.

First, different parts of the world may experience different kinds of environmental problems at varying levels of severity (Yearly 1996, pp.29–30). Yet, in most instances, constitutional environmental rights are phrased very broadly, with no particular problem singularly identified. Complicating the functional thesis further, some constitutions feature specific rights related to food, health, or water. This suggests that, for certain issues, states might respond to specific challenges with more narrowly circumscribed provisions. Perhaps even more revealingly, of the top 25 most water-stressed states, only *three* have constitutional environmental rights and *none* has rights to water (Boyd 2012; Reig et al. 2013). Thus, the likelihood that states adopt a relatively ambiguous catch-all provision as a direct means of rectifying environmental problems seems remote. This is not even to mention the impact that subtle variations in the phrasing might have on the types of protection afforded and the classes of persons who might enjoy the right (May & Daly 2015, p.84).

Second, there exist no studies evaluating the *long-term* effects of constitutional environmental rights on environmental performance. Schofer and Hironaka (2005) find that higher levels of structure, penetration, and persistence of *world society institutions* (e.g., not national constitutions) are associated with reductions in CO_2 and CFC emissions, common measures of environmental quality. More directly to the issue, Boyd (2012) presents a limited statistical analysis comparing the "ecological footprint" of countries with constitutional environmental rights against those without such rights at a single point in time (e.g., 2008). His results show that the former group enjoys smaller ecological footprints than the latter group. However, he rightfully counsels against drawing definitive conclusions from this preliminary assessment. Finally, Jeffords & Minkler (2016) offer what is arguably the most extensive effort to date seeking to assess the relationship between constitutional environmental rights and environmental outcomes. Using Yale's Environmental Performance Index and its constituent components as their measures of environmental quality, the authors determine that countries with constitutional environmental rights indeed experience higher levels of environmental performance than states without such rights on the books. Yet, the findings from this econometric study are limited by the fact that the environmental data included in the outcome measure only extend from 2000 to 2010 and the data set captures only 57 of the countries with constitutional environmental rights. Therefore, while recent empirical studies suggest that environmental rights may positively impact environmental outcomes, neither activists nor citizens nor leaders could have interpreted these rights, throughout the history of their existence in the international system, as empirically validated solutions for environmental problems.

Third, previous research on global trends in environmental policy adoption does not support the functionalist argument. Although recent studies demonstrate that higher levels of environmental degradation tend to lead to increased environmental concern among individuals (Givens & Jorgenson 2011; Knight & Messer 2012), less is known about the extent to which this concern translates into actual environmental laws or policies.[2] Scholarship from world society theorists, however, offers evidence that the presence of poor environmental conditions does not necessarily spur changes in environmental policy. As reported earlier, Hironaka (2002) finds that the diffusion of EIA legislation is significantly associated with international influences acting upon a state, but not levels of environmental degradation. Frank et al. (2007) conclude that ties to world society and the global environmental regime offer a better explanation for environmental policy reform in Asia than do the presence of domestic ENGOs or local environmental deterioration. The existence of national environmental policies reflects more than an acknowledgment regarding the state of the natural environment; their enactment depends on realistic appraisals of socioeconomic and institutional capacities as well (Sprinz & Vaahtoranta 1994, p.79). Thus, for the aforementioned reasons, I reject a functionalist explanation for the spread of constitutional environmental rights.

I also refute the possibility that hegemonic coercion plays a role in the adoption of constitutional environmental rights for two reasons. First, constitutional environmental rights are not likely to be among the major institutional reforms that powerful countries might compel states to adopt, mainly because there are more important governmental reforms to be implemented. In the case of the world's lone superpower, "environmental policy has never been central to the U.S. effort to create international order" (Falkner 2005, p.586). While the U.S. does champion the causes of democracy and human rights abroad, its motivation to force states to enact constitutional environmental rights seems opaque at best. A better case could be made for the promotion of procedural environmental rights, which are designed to enhance governmental transparency and democratic participation. Their implementation might also be easier to evaluate. To be sure, states rarely compel other states to enact environmental policies through military force (Lenschow et al. 2014, p.286).

Second, a proxy measurement of coercion is the extent to which weaker states follow the laws and policies of the powerful states. What seems like simple mimesis may in fact imply a rational calculation made by weaker states whereby the optimal strategy is to "engage in constitutional conformity as a means of currying favor with dominant states" (Law & Versteeg 2011, p.1178). However, many of the world's most powerful states—China, Germany, United Kingdom, and U.S.—do not have constitutional environmental rights at the federal level.

I argue that a theory of norm socialization offers more explanatory purchase than theories of domestic politics or rationalist–materialist considerations in understanding the global expansion of environmental rights for three reasons. First, the fact that countries whose constitutions feature environmental rights share little else of import suggests an explanation that lies beyond domestic circumstances. Second, the flexibility, specialization, and network capacity of transnational advocacy groups afford international norms related to world society the ability to transcend borders and become implanted in states throughout the international community. Finally, unlike procedural environmental rights, solidarity environmental rights present an unclear path to their fulfillment because they are ambiguously worded and rarely include specific instructions for implementation. These attributes imply that the bureaucratic, financial, and political costs of enacting constitutional environmental rights may be low, at least until transnational advocacy groups force the state into compliance. The minimal cost keeps the barriers to adoption low, leading to a greater likelihood that states that will entrench solidarity environmental rights in their constitutions as opposed to provisions of the procedural kind. Indeed, as Boyd (2012) indicates, states have adopted solidarity environmental rights over procedural environmental rights by a margin of more than three-to-one.

Research design

Hypotheses

In order to test the relative usefulness of the theories in terms of their ability to explain the observed trend, I translate the causal linkages described in the previous section into concrete, testable propositions. Specifically, I hypothesize the following:

H_1: The greater the number of international civil society organizations present in a state, the more likely a state will be to adopt environmental rights.

H_2: The greater the percentage of other countries in the region with environmental rights, the more likely it is that a country will adopt environmental rights.

H_3: The poorer a country's human rights legacy, the more likely it is to adopt environmental rights.

H_4: The greater a country's reliance on natural resources for its economic productivity, the less likely it is to adopt environmental rights.

H_5: The more external financial support a country receives, the more likely it is to adopt environmental rights.

H_6: The more democratic a country is, the more likely it is to adopt constitutional environmental rights.

H_1 is based on the idea that INGOs, serving as advocates of global human rights norms, urge states to adopt formal legal commitments to protect human rights regardless of the level of institutional support available to achieve compliance (Hafner-Burton & Tsutsui 2005, pp.1378, 1385). INGOs are transnational actors that "employ limited resources to make rules, set standards, propagate principles, and broadly represent 'humanity' vis-à-vis states and other actors" (Boli & Thomas 1999, p.14). Previous research demonstrates that governments placed in a negative spotlight are more likely to continue engaging in human rights abuses or increase violations of some human rights while reducing the incidence of abusing others (Hafner-Burton 2008). As an important distinction, the present analysis focuses on the enactment, not enforcement, of human rights. States, seeking to avoid being "named and shamed" by INGOs for not adequately addressing human rights issues and/or environmental concerns, will respond to the pressure by engaging in the relatively low-cost action of adopting a constitutional environmental right, bringing them into alignment with international society and reshaping their identity in the process.[3] This hypothesis rests on the suggestion that normative suasion can produce certain institutional reforms.[4]

H_2 is rooted in the notion that states within a given region may respond to the widespread instantiation of new norms in the area by following suit for reasons related to legitimation, conformity, and esteem (Finnemore & Sikkink 1998, p.903). Countries within the same geographic region may also tend toward isomorphism with regard to legal commitments due to socialization and policy transfer (Dolowitz & Marsh 2000) or possibly in order to avoid appearing like laggards and enhance their reputation to compete intra-regionally for investment (Simmons 2000, p.832). Regions are important objects of study because they help to explain why different geographic areas obtain heterogeneous outcomes, especially when attempting to understand variation in diffusion effects (Mainwaring & Pérez-Liñán 2005). States located in close proximity to one another may be more likely to share information and more likely to interact, prime conditions for the diffusion of innovations (Rogers 2003). In addition, states that are similar in "cultural, institutional and socio-economic terms are likely to develop similar policies as they may face similar problems" (Lenschow et al. 2014, p.288).

Countries writing new constitutions often borrow certain design elements from a limited number of exemplars (Osiatynski 2003, p.244) and many of the same people (e.g., foreign constitutional law scholars) who helped to write one new constitution within a region may be called upon to assist another country within the same geographic area. In addition, especially in the developing world, decision-makers in one region who participate in the creation of a new constitution may have all received the same special training from regional or international bodies working to promote democracy and development. Relatedly, countries within a given region may solicit expertise and technical advice from members of a relevant epistemic community during the constitution drafting process. An epistemic community refers to "a network of professionals with recognized expertise and competence in a particular domain and an authoritative claim to policy-relevant knowledge within that domain or issue area" (Haas 1992, p.3). American academics and consultants, acting as "constitutional Johnny Appleseeds" (Perry 1992, p.767), have long played an active role in drafting foreign constitutions, spreading legal models and U.S. legal ideas throughout Eastern Europe and beyond (deLisle 1999). Alternately, states may simply copy the provisions contained within the constitution of another country from within the region so that they do not appear to lack contemporary human rights laws that would make them seem less committed to the rule of law and human rights, and thus riskier prospects for foreign investment.

H_3 is suggested by the observation that countries with a history of insufficient protection of human rights, such as the former communist states in Eastern Europe, are more likely to adopt individual rights guarantees as a corrective measure (Osiatynski 1994, p.112). In this way, the promulgation of new human rights functions is a signal to the domestic polity that the state is dedicated to repairing relations with its citizenry, preventing backsliding from occurring, and promoting democratization through the enactment of progressive policies.

H_4 is predicated on the idea that a country that is highly dependent upon natural resources for its economic productivity will be less likely to develop strong governing institutions (Barbier 2005). Such countries may shy away from formalizing legal commitments that could be used to hamper the exploitation of natural resources in the event economic development results in environmental degradation that causes human rights to be violated.

H_5 is based on the empirical finding that countries dependent on external financial assistance will adopt certain institutional reforms to satisfy the demands of donor countries desiring to see such reforms implemented (Alesina & Dollar 2000, p.33). More precisely, the adoption of a constitutional environmental right may in fact serve as one element within a larger set of institutional reforms required under the terms of an aid package. In addition, countries may adopt environmental rights in order to appear committed to the protection of human rights and transparent for the purpose of attracting foreign investment (Law 2008, pp.46–48, 50).

H_6 relates to the argument that democracy and environmental conservation are inextricably linked (Shutkin 2000). As one theorist summarizes, "healthy communities cultivate both their social capital and their natural capital in public-spirited, participatory fashion" (Dryzek 2013, p.100). Thus, countries governed by democratic regimes should be more likely to facilitate the realization of popular environmental wants and needs through democratic means. In addition, democracy is associated with openness to global innovation, which includes international norms and "global environmental blueprints" (Frank et al. 2000, p.109). More broadly, the protection of human rights is considered an important element of good governance, and good governance remains strongly associated with democracy (Reif 2000, p.18). Therefore, countries that experience greater levels of democratic rule may be more inclined to entrench environmental rights in their respective governing charters.

A summary of the aforementioned hypotheses and the theories to which they apply is provided in Table 3.1.

Data

In this study I examine states across the time period from 1983 through 2010, nine years after the first constitutional environmental rights were enacted up through some of the most recent additions of countries with environmental rights (e.g., Dominican Republic and Kenya in 2010). This period allows for maximum coverage of the data sets selected. The unit of measurement is the country-year.

I analyze the relationship between six independent variables and one dependent variable. The first independent variable is international civil society influence (ICSI), which is measured by recording the number of INGOs with members in a particular state during a given year. Values range from 0 to over 64,000 organizations that might have a presence in a country. Annual data are extracted from the Union of International Associations' (UIA) (2012) *Yearbook of International Organizations, 2012–2013*. Previous researchers have found UIA's data "adequate for

Table 3.1 Hypotheses and the theory(ies) to which they correspond

Hypothesis	*Theory(ies)*
H_1: International Civil Society Influence	Norm Socialization
H_2: Regional Diffusion	Norm Socialization & Rationalism–Materialism
H_3: Human Rights Legacy	Domestic Politics
H_4: Natural Resource Dependency	Rationalism–Materialism
H_5: Monetary Influence	Norm Socialization & Rationalism–Materialism
H_6: Level of Democracy	Domestic Politics & Norm Socialization

meaningful analysis" (Boli & Thomas 1999, p.20). This variable serves as an indicator of norm socialization given the established role that INGOs play in disseminating international norms.

The second independent variable, regional diffusion (RD), is approximated by calculating the percentage of states within the geographic region in which a country is located, as defined by the World Bank, that have constitutional environmental rights in place in a given year. I determine the percentage of countries within a region that have environmental rights using data from the Comparative Constitutions Project[5] and Boyd (2012). This variable serves as a measure of the strength of the norm socialization and rationalism–materialism perspectives.

The third independent variable is human rights legacy (HRL). This variable is evaluated using a three-year moving average of a country's human rights record (e.g., in order to account for human rights performance in the recent past). Data pertaining to a country's human rights record are drawn from Freedom House, which provides country-level data on government respect for human rights from 1973 to 2012. I separately analyze two measures offered by Freedom House (2012)—political rights (PR) and civil liberties (CL), both scored on a scale from 1 (greatest level of protection afforded) to 7 (lowest level of protection afforded). Freedom House scores have been found to correlate highly with other popular measures of governance such as the Political Terror Scale (Anderson et al. 2002) and scholars have expressed confidence in their validity, especially in constitutional studies (Persson & Tabellini 2005). This variable captures an important factor relevant to the theory emphasizing domestic politics.

The fourth independent variable, natural resource dependency (NRD), is assessed using two different measures. First, I use World Bank data on the amount of total natural resource rents (NRR) a country obtains in a given year, expressed as a percentage of gross domestic product (GDP; 0–100 percent). These data represent the sum of a country's coal, forest, mineral, natural gas, and oil revenues earned in a given year. Second, I use World Bank data on agricultural land (AL), defined as the percentage of a country's land area that is arable, under permanent crops, and under permanent pastures (0–100 percent). These measures test the viability of rationalism–materialism in explaining the phenomenon observed.

The fifth independent variable, monetary incentives (MI), is estimated using three measures obtained from the World Bank. First, I use net bilateral aid (NBA) flows from Development Assistance Committee (DAC) donors in current U.S. dollars. Second, I use net inflows of FDI expressed as a percentage of GDP (0–100 percent). Third, I use net official development assistance (ODA) received expressed as a percentage of gross national income (GNI; 0–100 percent). These measures also serve as proxies for the theory based on rationalism–materialism.

The sixth independent variable, level of democracy (LD), is represented by regime characteristics (RC) scores from the Polity IV Project (Marshall & Jaggers 2012). Specifically, I use the Polity2 measure, a time-series analysis compatible version of the Polity measure, from Polity IV's Regime Characteristics and Transitions data set. Polity2 is a scale variable combining separate measures that capture the extent to which a country's governing regime tends toward autocracy or democracy. Values range from –10 (strongly autocratic) to +10 (strongly democratic). Specific regime categories include "autocracies" (–10 to –6), "anocracies" (–5 to +5), and democracies (+6 to +10). This variable speaks to the relevance of both domestic politics and norm socialization theories.

The dependent variable identifies the presence or absence of constitutional environmental rights in a country during a given year. For the purposes of measurement, a constitution is considered to include an environmental right if it features a likely justiciable[6] provision expressing the positive right of an individual to a(n) "clean" (Colombia Const., tit. II, ch. III, art. 79 (1991)), "ecologically balanced" (Timor-Leste Const., pt. II, tit. III, art. 61, § 1 (2002)), "healthy" (Chad Const., tit. II, ch. I, art. 47 (1996)), or "pleasant" (Korea Const., ch. II, art. 35, § 1 (1987)) environment (or some reasonable variant thereof).[7] Country-years in which an environmental right appears in a constitution are coded "1," while the absence of environmental rights during a given country-year is coded "0." I identify constitutional environmental rights using data from the Comparative Constitutions Project, specifically variable 627 [ENVREF_3], which codes for constitutions that include an environmental rights provision, and work by Boyd (2012).

In addition to the variables and measures listed above, I also utilize several control variables in the analysis—GDP, GDP per capita (GDPpc), land area (square kilometers; LA), population (POP), and population density (people per square kilometer of land area; PD). The data for all of the aforementioned controls come from the World Bank.

Method

I conduct statistical tests, specifically survival analysis,[8] in order to understand the relationship between various domestic and international factors and the presence or absence of environmental rights. Also referred to as "event history analysis" (Hutchison 1988, p.206), survival analysis is a tool social scientists use to better understand what influences the duration and timing of important events (Box-Steffensmeier & Jones 1997), like the passage of a new constitution. I employ a particular method known as the Cox model,[9] which is well suited to handle data with binary outcomes and time-dependent variables, making it an ideal statistical technique for the current endeavor. It is also commonly employed in empirical research on world society theory in sociology (Frank 1997; Meyer et al. 1997b; Frank et al. 2000, 2007; Hironaka 2002). Using this model I analyze variation in the times-to-event (e.g., promulgation of a constitutional environmental right) across countries for the six independent variables described earlier.

Results

Due to the utilization of different sources of data in this study and the unique features of each data set, I follow two approaches to the statistical analysis—one that maximizes the number of cases analyzed and another that maximizes the number of variables tested.[10] In the maximum-case model, five measures—civil liberties, GDP per capita, international civil society influence, population density, and regime characteristics—were found to produce a statistically significant effect on the likelihood that a country will adopt a constitutional environmental right.[11] The statistical output from this model is included in Table 3.2.[12]

The hazard ratio for CL suggests that with every one-unit increase in a country's CL score (e.g., citizens are less free from violations of their civil liberties), the likelihood that a country will entrench a constitutional environmental right in its governing charter *increases* by 38 percent. The hazard ratio for GDPpc signifies that with an increase of $100 in a country's GDPpc, the likelihood that the country will adopt a constitutional environmental right *decreases* by 1 percent. The hazard ratio for ICSI suggests that for every 100 INGOs with a membership presence in a country, the likelihood that a state enacts a constitutional environmental right *increases* by 8 percent. The hazard ratio for PD indicates that with the addition of 100 people per square kilometer, the likelihood that a country promulgates a constitutional environmental right *decreases* by 1 percent. Finally, the hazard ratio for RC reports that for every one-unit increase in a country's Polity IV score (e.g., a country tends more toward democracy than autocracy), the likelihood that such a country will instantiate an environmental right in its constitution *increases* by 16 percent. In the maximum-case model, countries that scored +3 or higher on the Polity IV scale were *128 percent more likely* to enact a constitutional environmental right than

Table 3.2 Statistical output from the maximum-case model

Measure	*Hazard Ratio*	*SE*	*Z-score*
Civil Liberties	1.38*	.21	2.09
GDP per capita	0.99*	.00	−3.33
International Civil Society Influence	1.08*	.03	2.57
Population Density	0.99*	.00	−3.71
Regime Characteristics	1.16*	.05	3.68

Note: SE = standard error. Number of observations = 3245. * $p < .05$.

countries that scored +2 or lower. This result suggests that developing countries in the process of democratization may be the most likely group of states to constitutionalize environmental rights.

In the maximum-variable model only four of the measures—GDPpc, NBA, PD, and RC—were found to be statistically significant at the .05 level.[13] The results of the analysis for this model are depicted below in Table 3.3.

The hazard ratio for GDPpc indicates that with an increase of $100 in a country's GDPpc in a given year, the likelihood that the country will adopt a constitutional environmental right *decreases* by 2 percent. The hazard ratio for NBA, while significant, is not empirically informative because the statistic suggests that the effect of the measure is virtually nonexistent.[14] The hazard ratio for PD signifies that with the addition of 100 people per square kilometer, the likelihood that a country enacts a constitutional environmental right *decreases* by 48 percent. Finally, the hazard ratio for RC demonstrates that for every one-unit increase in a country's Polity IV score, the likelihood that a country will incorporate an environmental rights provision into its constitution *increases* by 10 percent. In addition, countries that scored +2 or above were *184 percent more likely* to entrench a solidarity environmental right in their constitution.[15]

Discussion

The results of the statistical analysis[16] with respect to the hypotheses enumerated earlier are summarized in Table 3.4.

Table 3.3 Statistical output from the maximum-variable model

Measure	*Hazard Ratio*	*SE*	*Z-score*
Agricultural Land	.99	.01	–.12
Civil Liberties	.94	.27	–.23
Foreign Direct Investment	.98	.02	–.75
Gross Domestic Product	1.00	2.44e-12	1.42
GDP per capita	.98*	–.02	–2.10
International Civil Society Influence	1.09	.07	1.34
Land Area	1.00	1.57e-07	.77
Net Bilateral Aid	1.00*	5.24e-11	3.06
Net Official Development Assistance	.98	.02	–1.24
Political Rights	1.36	.33	1.27
Population	1.00	1.05e-08	–1.58
Population Density	.52*	–.01	–2.94
Regime Characteristics	1.10*	.09	3.20
Regional Diffusion	.99	.01	–.92
Total Natural Resource Rents	1.01	.01	.69

Note: SE = standard error. Number of observations = 2563. * $p < .05$.

Table 3.4 Evaluation of hypotheses

Hypothesis	*Result*
H_1: International Civil Society Influence	Support
H_2: Regional Diffusion	No Support
H_3: Human Rights Legacy	Partial Support
H_4: Natural Resource Dependency	No Support
H_5: Monetary Influence	No Support
H_6: Level of Democracy	Strong Support

First, the analysis suggests that countries with greater levels of international civil society involvement are more likely to adopt a constitutional environmental right. Second, globally speaking, the enactment of environmental rights does not appear to be influenced by the extent to which such rights have been constitutionalized elsewhere in a given region.[17] Third, in accordance with expectations, I find that countries with a history of poor human rights practices are more likely to promulgate a constitutional environmental right. Fourth, the extent to which a country's economy depends upon natural resources is not meaningfully related to the presence of environmental rights. Fifth, the degree to which a country relies on foreign financial assistance did not have an impact on a state's propensity to offer constitutional protection for environmental rights.[18] Sixth, as anticipated in the final hypothesis, democracies are more likely than their autocratic brethren to entrench environmental rights in national constitutions.

The statistical analysis conducted in this study provides the greatest support for explanations based on domestic politics and norm socialization (see Table 3.5).

The results suggest that the presence of INGOs in a country plays an important role in the introduction of ideas, networks, resources, and leadership necessary to promote and institutionalize emerging norms of world society. In-depth case study analyses will be required to determine the precise mechanisms by which INGOs successfully integrate new norms, such as environmental rights, into new and existing governing institutions,

Table 3.5 Evaluation of theoretical explanations

Theory	*Result*
Norm Socialization	Support
Rationalism–Materialism	No Support
Domestic Politics	Support

especially in developing countries where resources are scarce. The high degree of support obtained for the theory of domestic politics suggests that the global emergence of constitutional environmental rights is influenced by conditions internal to the state. While more structured, focused comparisons are better positioned to tease out the causal mechanisms at work in this phenomenon, the findings produced here bolster the claim of analysts who argue that domestic conditions affect a state's receptiveness to international norms (Checkel 1999). As a state's level of democracy proved to be the most consistently supported variable, it stands to reason that perhaps the relationship between democracy and openness to global innovation (Frank et al. 2000, p.109) is a rather significant factor in the process of designing a constitution. Finally, as predicted earlier, the possibility of hegemonic coercion, a dimension of the rationalist–materialist theory approximated by analyzing the effect of foreign aid dependence, did not bear fruit.

In addition to examining the variables of interest, several control variables were tested. Of those controls included in the analysis, GDPpc and PD proved statistically significant. Specifically, countries with a lower GDPpc and lower PD were more likely to adopt constitutional environmental rights. These results suggest that constitutional environmental rights are more common among less-crowded developing countries. Although the theoretical basis for this finding is not immediately forthcoming, one might surmise that the push to entrench environmental rights is greater in places where the landscape is less obstructed by urban development, and individuals both prize the preservation of their open spaces and are more aware of changes to their natural environment. However, this logic may seem counterintuitive given that people in rural areas consistently exhibit lower levels of concern for environmental quality than people in urban areas (Lowe & Pinhey 1982).

Recent research on constitutional convergence inspired further statistical analysis. In particular, I examined the relationship between comprehensiveness (e.g., number of rights appearing in a constitution), ideology (e.g., degree to which a constitution reflects either a libertarian [negative rights] or statist [positive rights] orientation), legal tradition, and the presence or absence of constitutional environmental rights. Using panel data from Law & Versteeg (2011) and La Porta et al. (1999), I ran three logistic regression models. The results demonstrate that constitutions with environmental rights are significantly more likely to include a greater number of rights and reflect a statist ideology.[19] In addition, despite previous research concluding that countries with the same legal tradition adopt similar constitutional rights (Goderis & Versteeg 2013; Gutmann et al. 2013), my analysis suggests that legal tradition is not a significant predictor of the likelihood that a country will adopt constitutional environmental rights.[20] Although states with French and socialist legal traditions constitute over 80 percent of the countries with constitutional environmental rights,[21] the trend is continuously expanding within other legal traditions.[22]

Countries that have yet to adopt constitutional environmental rights may be reluctant to do so for at least two reasons. First, rather than being laggards, these countries may have positioned themselves to simply "wait and see" the effects of including these kinds of provisions in constitutions. This perspective rests on the premise that it is best to observe how these situations play out in other states before promulgating an environmental right in one's home constitution. Some countries may wait in order to observe the experience of those states with constitutional environmental rights (e.g., number of cases filed, number of issues resolved, costs of litigation, effectiveness of enabling legislation, etc.) before deciding to enact such a right. As the data set for this analysis ended with the year 2010, more countries may adopt constitutional environmental rights in a new constitution or as an amendment to an existing constitution in the near future.[23]

Second, some developing states may have deliberately avoided instantiating environmental rights in their respective constitutions given the lack of resources these countries have to adequately protect such a broad right. Resources necessary to the successful protection of an environmental right may include an environmental agency with sufficient personnel, budget, and discretion to investigate environmental problems; a legal system with the capacity and integrity to adjudicate cases involving environmental harms committed by state and private actors; and well-functioning organizations with the financial capacity to help bring cases on behalf of marginalized and indigent members of society who would otherwise have little legal recourse to the alleged violations of their constitutional rights. It may be the case that some countries establish an environmental agency to oversee the implementation of environmental objectives but do not have constitutional environmental rights. However, in some instances the converse may also be true. That is, countries might adopt a constitutional environmental right absent the institutional resources necessary to fulfill the legal imperative. More research is needed to determine the motive(s) behind pursuing one or more avenues for protecting environmental rights.

Conclusion

This chapter presents the results of a global quantitative analysis designed to test three theoretical explanations for the worldwide expansion of constitutional environmental rights—domestic politics, norm socialization, and rationalism–materialism. Using the statistical technique known as survival analysis, I found that constitutional environmental rights are more likely to emerge in countries with a greater presence of international civil society organizations, a poorer record of human rights practices, and higher levels of democratic governance. These findings offer support for explanations based on domestic politics and norm socialization, but not rationalist–materialist considerations. That is, states constitutionalize environmental rights for reasons relating to the quality of domestic governing institutions and the normative influence of international civil society, not concerns about competing for foreign aid or preserving lucrative natural resources. Further research on the topic would benefit by improving the coverage and quality of data used to operationalize relevant theoretical perspectives and testing new variables, such as the adoption of international treaties, the presence of ENGOs, or judicial independence, which may offer additional explanatory value. In the following chapter, I present a comparative study of constitutional design in Nepal and Sri Lanka devised to uncover factors affecting the likelihood of adoption that were unaccounted for in the statistical analysis.

Notes

1 The very process of adopting a constitution is argued to have a legitimating effect. Indeed, one observer characterizes constitutionalism as "a passport to international acceptability" (Klug 2000, p.48).

2 Some notable work on environmental policy-making in the U.S., however, shows that public opinion indeed influences political outcomes related to environmental issues (Brace et al. 2002; Johnson et al. 2005; Jarvis 2008; Anderson 2011).

3 Here I extend Hathaway's argument regarding the reasons why a country might ratify a human rights treaty to the adoption of a constitutional environmental right: "where compliance is least likely, commitment is often relatively costless" (Hathaway 2007, p.613).

4 I chose to operationalize norm socialization in terms of international civil society influence and not another measure like whether or not a country is a signatory to a human rights treaty because there is no international human rights agreement featuring the right to a healthy environment (Shelton 2006, p.166), and without a legally binding requirement compelling states to adopt such a provision there exists no direct international pressure to transpose such a right into national legal systems (Pesendorfer 2014, p.213).

5 The Comparative Constitutions Project can be accessed at www.comparativeconstitutionsproject.org.

6 I consider a constitutional environmental right to be justiciable if it is located in a part of the constitution, such as a section on fundamental rights, which is typically viewed as possessing authoritative legal status. Environmental rights provisions appearing in preambles are most often not justiciable, except in cases where subsequent portions of the constitution stipulate otherwise. Generally speaking, justiciability of constitutional rights depends on the extent to which they can be enforced through a country's domestic legal system (May & Daly 2015, p.102).

7 This coding scheme is designed to differentiate a constitutional environmental right from related substantive rights (e.g., "the right to health") and procedural environmental rights (e.g., "the right to information about the environment").

8 Political science researchers have shown that survival analysis is better equipped than ordinary logit or probit statistical models to analyze time-series, cross-section data with binary outcomes given the likelihood that the observations will be temporally related (Beck et al. 1998).

9 Also known as the proportional hazards model or Cox regression model, this model is semi-parametric in that the model is based on the assumption of proportional hazards, although no particular form of probability distribution is assumed for the survival times (Collett 2003, p.56).

10 First, I conduct an analysis oriented toward maximizing the number of *cases* included. This necessarily entails removing those measures and variables that suffer from severe missingness, which I construe as a condition in which greater than 5 percent of the data is absent. All variables (with the exception of RD) are initially treated with extrapolation in order to fill in missing values of the data, but those measures for which the number of missing data exceeded 5 percent are excluded from the model. The employment of this strategy resulted in the removal of four measures featured in the full model—FDI (6.9 percent missing data), NRD (5.2 percent missing data), NBA (22.2 percent missing data), and ODA (38.6 percent missing data). Next, I use backward elimination to remove additional measures that fail to achieve statistical significance at the .05 level. This procedure resulted in the elimination of six additional measures. This approach to model selection allowed me to retain 148 total cases, 62 of the original 75 cases in which constitutional environmental rights were adopted, and five statistically significant variables. Second, because it is necessary to test the full model, I conduct another analysis focused on maximizing the number of *variables* to be tested. Again, all measures are subjected to extrapolation prior to the removal of any cases. This process requires the deletion of cases that suffer from severe missingness, here identified as a situation in which a case lacks data for 50 percent or more of the years under observation on any given measure. Upon completing the removal of cases with severe missingness, the data set was comprised of 113 total cases, 45 of the original 75 cases in which constitutional environmental rights were adopted, and all 15 measures in the full model. Next, in order to construct the most robust statistical model, I follow the four-step model selection procedure advocated by Collett (2003, pp.80–83). In the first step, I run a Cox model regression for each of the 15 measures independently. In the second step, I retain only those measures that produce both statistically significant results and a log-likelihood value one-unit or more greater than the log-likelihood for the null model. Then I compute the change in the value of the log-likelihood for the tested model when I omit, one at a time, each of the previously retained measures. In the third step, I reintroduce, one by one, each of the measures I discarded at the beginning of step two to observe whether bringing back any of these measures produces a one-unit or greater improvement in the log-likelihood of the tested model. Three such measures, each statistically significant at the .10 level, were identified. In the fourth step, I conduct a final model check by running Cox model regressions on three models, each of which includes a different pairing of two of the measures brought back into the analysis in step three. The log-likelihoods of each of these paired analyses are then compared to the log-likelihood for the model tested with all seven measures. The purpose here is to determine whether omitting any of the reacquired measures causes a significant decrease (e.g., reduction in model skill) in the log-likelihood of the tested model. The two model selection methods described above are employed in order to balance the competing interests of case maximization and variable maximization. The two strategies produced fairly consistent results, thus allowing for greater confidence in the validity of the conclusions subsequently drawn from the analysis.

11 Values for the GDPpc, ICSI, and PD measures were adjusted by dividing each observation by 100 in order to improve the interpretability of the results.

12 Several interactions, along with the introduction of a linear spline to the model equation, were tested, but none yielded statistically significant results. Using Stata's stepwise function, which eliminates variables that exceed p-values of 0.05, the following measures were excluded from the resulting full model: AL, GDP, LA, PR, POP, and RD. The full statistical output from the maximum-case model is on file with the author.

13 The three measures not included in the final model were FDI ($z = -1.48$), ICSI ($z = 1.64$), and PR ($z = 1.56$).

14 Indeed, the standard error of the NBA measure was 5.24e-11 and the 95 percent confidence interval was (1, 1).

15 It is important to note that despite the use of all variables and measures for which data were collected and included in the initial version of this model, the fact that this model was analyzed using 24 percent fewer total cases and 27 percent fewer cases in which constitutional environmental rights were enacted than the maximum-case model likely reduced the overall model skill by a non-trivial amount.

16 Upon completing the analysis, I conducted diagnostic tests on both the maximum-case and maximum-variable models to establish whether or not the major assumption underlying the Cox model—that of proportional hazards—had been violated. In particular, I conducted two kinds of tests: (1) visual assessments of graphic plots and (2) Chi-square tests comparing model output with the Schoenfeld residuals of the data. To develop plots for both models, the median values for each of the measures were calculated and dummy variables were created to separate observations above (coded "1") and below (coded "0") the median. Then, each measure was plotted in three ways: (1) separately using the dummy variable in a log-log plot; (2) adjusted for the presence of the other statistically significant measures in a dummy variable log-log plot; and (3) separately in a survivor plot. For the maximum-case model, the plots did not show evidence that the proportional hazards assumption had been violated. Similarly, for the maximum-variable model, a visual inspection of the plots failed to reveal any obvious departures from the proportional hazards assumption. Chi-square tests were conducted by comparing the observed values against the Schoenfeld residuals in order to discern whether or not the null hypothesis—that the hazard rate between the two groups does not differ—can be rejected. With the exception of the ICSI variable, all of the other measures obtained Chi-square values that preclude rejecting the null hypothesis, meaning that it is likely that the proportional hazards assumption was not violated.

17 In an analysis of potential diffusion effects within the three regions of the world in which environmental rights are most prevalent, Gellers (2012) finds that the extent of constitutional environmental rights present in a given region *negatively* impacts the likelihood that such rights will subsequently be enacted elsewhere in the area.

18 Only one measure of the MI variable proved to be statistically significant and its hazard ratio did not indicate a positive or negative effect on the outcome of interest.

19 Results are on file with the author.

20 These results are reported in Appendix B in Gellers (2015).

21 Author's own calculations.

22 In the past five years (2011–2015), four out of the nine states that have adopted constitutional environmental rights—Jamaica (2011), South Sudan (2011), Fiji (2013), and Zimbabwe (2013)—feature non-French/socialist legal traditions (all English, except for Zimbabwe, which is Roman Dutch and English).

23 Since this analysis was conducted, Jamaica (2011), Morocco (2011), South

Sudan (2011), Mauritania (2012), Fiji (2013), Zimbabwe (2013), Vietnam (2013), Tunisia (2014), and Egypt (2014) have become the latest countries to formally adopt constitutional environmental rights.

Bibliography

Abrams, B.A. & Lewis, K.A., 1993. Human Rights and the Distribution of U.S. Foreign Aid. *Public Choice*, 77(4), pp.815–821.

Ackerman, B., 1997. The Rise of World Constitutionalism. *Virginia Law Review*, 83, pp.771–797.

Agnone, J., 2007. Amplifying Public Opinion: The Policy Impact of the U.S. Environmental Movement. *Social Forces*, 85(4), pp.1593–1620.

Alesina, A. & Dollar, D., 2000. Who Gives Foreign Aid to Whom and Why? *Journal of Economic Growth*, 5(1), pp.33–63.

Anderson, C.J., Regan, P.M. & Ostergard, R.L., 2002. Political Repression and Public Perceptions of Human Rights. *Political Research Quarterly*, 55(2), pp.439–456.

Anderson, S.E., 2011. Complex Constituencies: Intense Environmentalists and Representation. *Environmental Politics*, 20(4), pp.547–565.

Bándi, G., 1992. The Right to Environment in Theory and Practice: The Hungarian Experience. *Connecticut Journal of International Law*, 8, pp.439–466.

Barbier, E., 2005. *Natural Resources and Economic Development*, Cambridge: Cambridge University Press.

Beck, N., Katz, J.N. & Tucker, R., 1998. Taking Time Seriously: Time-Series-Cross-Section Analysis with a Binary Dependent Variable. *American Journal of Political Science*, 42(4), pp.1260–1288.

Blanton, S.L. & Blanton, R.G., 2006. Human Rights and Foreign Direct Investment. *Business and Society*, 45(4), pp.464–485.

Boli, J., 1999. Conclusion: World Authority Structures and Legitimations. In J. Boli & G. M. Thomas, eds. *Constructing World Culture: International Nongovernmental Organizations Since 1875*. Stanford: Stanford University Press, pp.267–300.

Boli, J. & Thomas, G.M., 1999. INGOs and the Orgnanization of World Culture. In J. Boli & G. M. Thomas, eds. *Constructing World Culture: International Nongovernmental Organizations Since 1875*. Stanford: Stanford University Press, pp.13–49.

Box-Steffensmeier, J.M. & Jones, B.S., 1997. Time is of the Essence: Event History Models in Political Science. *American Journal of Political Science*, 41(4), pp.1414–1461.

Boyd, D.R., 2012. *The Environmental Rights Revolution: A Global Study of Constitutions, Human Rights, and the Environment*. Vancouver, BC: UBC Press.

Brace, P., Sims-Butler, K., Arceneaux, K., & Johnson, M., 2002. Public Opinion in the American States: New Perspectives Using National Survey Data. *American Journal of Political Science*, 46(1), pp.173–189.

Brandl, E. & Bungert, H., 1992. Constitutional Entrenchment of Environmental Protection: A Comparative Analysis of Experiences Abroad. *Harvard Environmental Law Review*, 16, pp.1–100.

Brechin, S.R., 1999. Objective Problems, Subjective Values, and Global Environmentalism: Evaluating the Postmaterialist Argument and Challenging a New Explanation. *Social Science Quarterly*, 80(4), pp.793–809.

Busse, M. & Hefeker, C., 2007. Political Risk, Institutions and Foreign Direct Investment. *European Journal of Political Economy*, 23(2), pp.397–415.

Calvert, J.W., 1979. The Social and Ideological Bases of Support for Environmental Legislation: An Examination of Public Attitudes and Legislative Action. *The Western Political Quarterly*, 32(3), pp.327–337.

Cardenas, S., 2004. Norm Collision: Explaining the Effects of International Human Rights Pressure on State Behavior. *International Studies Review*, 6(2), pp.213–232.

Chad Const., tit. II, ch. I, art. 47 (1996).

Checkel, J., 1999. Norms, Institutions, and National Identity in Contemporary Europe. *International Studies Quarterly*, 43(1), pp.84–114.

Collett, D., 2003. *Modelling Survival Data in Medical Research*. 2nd ed., Boca Raton: Chapman & Hall/CRC.

Colombia Const., tit. II, ch. III, art. 79 (1991).

Compagnon, D., Chan, S. & Mert, A., 2012. The Changing Role of the State. In F. Biermann & P. Pattberg, eds. *Global Environmental Governance Reconsidered*. Cambridge: MIT Press, pp.237–263.

deLisle, J., 1999. Lex Americana?: United States Legal Assistance, American Legal Models, and Legal Change in the Post-Communist World and Beyond. *University of Pennsylvania Journal of International Economic Law*, 20(2), pp.179–308.

Dolowitz, D.P. & Marsh, D., 2000. Learning from Abroad: The Role of Policy Transfer in Contemporary Policy-Making. *Governance*, 13(1), pp.5–23.

Dryzek, J.S., 2013. *The Politics of the Earth: Environmental Discourses*. 3rd ed., Oxford: Oxford University Press.

Duchacek, I.D., 1968. National Constitutions: A Functional Approach. *Comparative Politics*, 1(1), pp.91–102.

Epp, C.R., 1998. *The Rights Revolution: Lawyers, Activists, and Supreme Courts in Comparative Perspective*. Chicago: University of Chicago Press.

Falkner, R., 2005. American Hegemony and the Global Environment. *International Studies Review*, 7(4), pp.585–599.

Farber, D.A., 2002. Rights as Signals. *The Journal of Legal Studies*, 31(1), pp.83–98.

Feldman, N., 2005. Imposed Constitutionalism. *Connecticut Law Review*, 37(4), pp.857–890.

Fernandes, E., 1996. Constitutional Environmental Rights in Brazil. In A.E. Boyle & M.R. Anderson, eds. *Human Rights Approaches to Environmental Protection*. Oxford: Clarendon Press, pp.265–284.

Finnemore, M. & Sikkink, K., 1998. International Norm Dynamics and Political Change. *International Organization*, 52(4), pp.887–917.

Frank, D.J., 1997. Science, Nature, and the Globalization of the Environment, 1870–1990. *Social Forces*, 76(2), pp.409–437.

Frank, D.J., Hironaka, A. & Schofer, E., 2000. The Nation-State and the Natural Environment over the Twentieth Century. *American Sociological Review*, 65, pp.96–116.

Frank, D.J., Longhofer, W. & Schofer, E., 2007. World Society, NGOs, and Environmental Policy Reform in Asia. *International Journal of Comparative Sociology*, 48(4), pp.275–295.

Freedom House, 2012. *Freedom in the World 2012*, Available at: www.freedomhouse.org/report-types/freedom-world [Accessed December 14, 2013].

Gellers, J.C., 2012. Greening Constitutions with Environmental Rights: Testing the Isomorphism Thesis. *Review of Policy Research*, 29(4), pp.523–543.

Gellers, J.C., 2015. Explaining the Emergence of Constitutional Environmental Rights: A Global Quantitative Analysis. *Journal of Human Rights and the Environment*, 6(1), pp.75–97.

Ginsburg, T., Elkins, Z. & Blount, J., 2009. Does the Process of Constitution-Making Matter? *Annual Review of Law and Social Science*, 5, pp.201–223.

Givens, J.E. & Jorgenson, A.K., 2011. The Effects of Affluence, Economic Development, and Environmental Degradation on Environmental Concern: A Multilevel Analysis. *Organization & Environment*, 24(1), pp.74–91.

Goderis, B. & Versteeg, M., 2013. Transnational Constitutions, *Social Science Research Network*. Available at: http://papers.ssrn.com/abstract=2216582 [Accessed December 14, 2013].

Gravelle, R.K., 1997. Enforcing the Elusive: Environmental Rights in East European Constitutions. *Virginia Environmental Law Journal*, 16, pp.633–660.

Gutmann, J., Imhof, S. & Voigt, S., 2013. Are You Green Yet? On the Diffusion of Constitutionally Protected Environmental Rights. *Social Science Research Network*. Available at: http://papers.ssrn.com/abstract=2311421 [Accessed November 14, 2013].

Haas, P.M., 1992. Introduction: Epistemic Communities and International Policy Coordination. *International Organization*, 46(1), pp.1–35.

Hafner-Burton, E.M., 2008. Sticks and Stones: Naming and Shaming the Human Rights Enforcement Problem. *International Organization*, 62, pp.689–716.

Hafner-Burton, E.M. & Tsutsui, K., 2005. Human Rights in a Globalizing World: The Paradox of Empty Promises. *American Journal of Sociology*, 110(5), pp.1373–1411.

Hancock, J., 2003. *Environmental Human Rights: Power, Ethics, and Law*. Burlington, VT: Ashgate.

Hathaway, O.A., 2007. Why Do Countries Commit to Human Rights Treaties? *Journal of Conflict Resolution*, 51(4), pp.588–621.

Henckaerts, J.-M. & Van der Jeught, S., 1998. Human Rights Protection Under the New Constitutions of Central Europe. *Loyola L.A. International and Comparative Law Journal*, 20, pp.475–506.

Hironaka, A., 2002. The Globalization of Environmental Protection: The Case of Environmental Impact Assessment. *International Journal of Comparative Sociology*, 43(1), pp.65–78.

Hutchison, D., 1988. Event History and Survival Analysis in the Social Sciences. *Quality & Quantity*, 22, pp.203–219.

Ikenberry, G.J. & Kupchan, C.A., 1990. Socialization and Hegemonic Power. *International Organization*, 44(3), pp.283–315.

Jarvis, H.E., 2008. *Public Opinion and the Introduction of Congressional Environmental Legislation, 1973–2002*. Master's Thesis. University of South Florida.

Jeffords, C. & Minkler, L., 2016. Do Constitutions Matter? The Effects of Constitutional Environmental Rights Provisions on Environmental Outcomes. *Kyklos*, 69(2), pp.294–335.

Johnson, M., Brace, P. & Arceneaux, K., 2005. Public Opinion and Dynamic Representation in the American States: The Case of Environmental Attitudes. *Social Science Quarterly*, 86(1), pp.87–108.

Keck, M.E. & Sikkink, K., 1998. *Activists Beyond Borders: Advocacy Networks in International Politics*. Ithaca, NY: Cornell University Press.

Keck, M.E. & Sikkink, K., 1999. Transnational Advocacy Networks in International and Regional Politics. *International Social Science Journal*, 51(159), pp.89–101.

Klug, H., 2000. *Constituting Democracy: Law, Globalism and South Africa's Political Reconstruction*. Cambridge: Cambridge University Press.

Knight, K.W. & Messer, B.L., 2012. Environmental Concern in Cross-National Perspective: The Effects of Affluence, Environmental Degradation, and World Society. *Social Science Quarterly*, 93(2), pp.521–537.

Korea Const., ch. II, art. 35, § 1 (1987).

La Porta, R., Lopez-de-Silanes, F., Shleifer, A., & Vishny, R., 1999. The Quality of Government. *Journal of Law, Economics, and Organization*, 15(1), pp.222–279.

Law, D.S., 2008. Globalization and the Future of Constitutional Rights. *Northwestern University Law Review*, 102(3), pp.1–89.

Law, D.S. & Versteeg, M., 2011. The Evolution and Ideology of Global Constitutionalism. *California Law Review*, 99(5), pp.1163–1254.

Lenschow, A., Liefferink, D. & Jörgens, H., 2014. Complex Causation in Cross-National Environmental Policy Convergence. In H. Jörgens, A. Lenschow, & D. Liefferink, eds. *Understanding Environmental Policy Convergence: The Power of Words, Rules and Money*. New York: Cambridge University Press, pp.265–295.

Lieberman, E.S., 2005. Nested Analysis as a Mixed-Method Strategy for Comparative Research. *American Political Science Review*, 99(3), pp.435–452.

Lowe, G.D. & Pinhey, T.K., 1982. Rural-Urban Differences in Support for Environmental Protection. *Rural Sociology*, 47(1), pp.114–128.

Mainwaring, S. & Pérez-Liñán, A., 2005. *Why Regions of the World are Important: Regional Specificities and Region-Wide Diffusion of Democracy*. Kellogg Institute, University of Notre Dame. Available at: https://pdfs.semanticscholar.org/0dd4/35970c1516d66d55c9b684a9baaa24c99def.pdf [Accessed April 22, 2014].

Marshall, M.G. & Jaggers, K., 2012. *Polity IV Project: Political Regime Characteristics and Transitions, 1800–2012*. College Park: Center for International Development and Conflict Management. Available at: www.systemicpeace.org/polity/polity4.htm [Accessed December 14, 2013].

May, J.R. & Daly, E., 2015. *Global Environmental Constitutionalism*. Cambridge: Cambridge University Press.

Meijerink, S. & Huitema, D., 2010. Policy Entrepreneurs and Change Strategies: Lessons from Sixteen Case Studies of Water Transitions Around the Globe. *Ecology and Society*, 15(2), p.21.

Meyer, J.W., Boli, J., Thomas, G.M., & Ramirez, F.O., 1997a. World Society and the Nation–State. *American Journal of Sociology*, 103(1), pp.144–181.

Meyer, J.W., Frank, D.J., Hironaka, A., Schofer, E., & Tuma, N.B., 1997b. The Structuring of a World Environmental Regime, 1870-1990. *International Organization*, 51(4), pp.623–651.

Mol, A.P.J., 2002. Ecological Modernization and the Global Economy. *Global Environmental Politics*, 2(2), pp.92–115.

Olson, M., 1965. *The Logic of Collective Action: Public Goods and the Theory of Groups*. Cambridge: Harvard University Press.

Osiatynski, W., 1994. Rights in New Constitutions of East Central Europe. *Columbia Human Rights Law Review*, 26, pp.111–166.

Osiatynski, W., 2003. Paradoxes of Constitutional Borrowing. *International Journal of Constitutional Law*, 1(2), pp.244–268.

Perry, B., 1992. Constitutional Johnny Appleseeds: American Consultants and the Drafting of Foreign Constitutions. *Albany Law Review*, 55, pp.767–792.

Persson, T. & Tabellini, G.E., 2005. *The Economic Effects of Constitutions*. Cambridge: MIT Press.

Pesendorfer, D., 2014. Converging Ideas About Risk Regulation? The Precautionary Principle in National Legal Systems. In H. Jörgens, A. Lenschow, & D. Liefferink, eds. *Understanding Environmental Policy Convergence: The Power of Words, Rules and Money*. New York: Cambridge University Press, pp.209–236.

Petrović-Randjelović, M., 2007. Foreign Direct Investment and Sustainable Development: An Analysis of the Impact of Environmental Regulations on Investment Location Decisions. *Facta Universitatis – Series: Economics and Organization*, 4(2), pp.183–190.

Pierson, P., 2000. The Limits of Design: Explaining Institutional Origins and Change. *Governance*, 13(4), pp.475–499.

Popović, N., 1996. Pursuing Environmental Justice with International Human Rights and State Constitutions. *Stanford Environmental Law Journal*, 15, pp.338–376.

Price, R., 1998. Reversing the Gun Sights: Transnational Civil Society Targets Land Mines. *International Organization*, 52(3), pp.613–644.

Reif, L.C., 2000. Building Democratic Institutions: The Role of National Human Rights Institutions in Good Governance and Human Rights Protection. *Harvard Human Rights Journal*, 13, pp.1–70.

Reig, P., Maddocks, A. & Gassert, F., 2013. World's 37 Most Water-Stressed Countries. World Resources Institute. Available at: www.wri.org/blog/world%E2%80%99s-37-most-water-stressed-countries [Accessed December 21, 2013].

Richards, D.L., Gelleny, R.D. & Sacko, D.H., 2001. Money with a Mean Streak? Foreign Economic Penetration and Government Respect for Human Rights in Developing Countries. *International Studies Quarterly*, 45(2), pp.219–239.

Risse, T. & Sikkink, K., 1999. The Socialization of International Human Rights Norms into Domestic Practices: Introduction. In T. Risse, S.C. Ropp, & K. Sikkink, eds. *The Power of Human Rights: International Norms and Domestic Change*. Cambridge: Cambridge University Press, pp.1–38.

Rogers, E.M., 2003. *Diffusion of Innovation*. 5th ed., Glencoe: Free Press.

Rucht, D., 1999. The Impact of Environmental Movements in Western Societies. In M. Giugni, D. McAdam, & C. Tilly, eds. *How Social Movements Matter*. Minneapolis: University of Minnesota Press, pp.204–224.

Schofer, E. & Hironaka, A., 2005. The Effects of World Society on Environmental Protection Outcomes. *Social Forces*, 84(1), pp.25–47.

Shelton, D., 1991. Human Rights, Environmental Rights, and the Right to Environment. *Stanford Journal of International Law*, 28, pp.103–138.

Shelton, D., 2006. Human Rights and the Environment: What Specific Environmental Rights Have Been Recognized? *Denver Journal of International Law and Policy*, 35, pp.129–171.

Shutkin, W.A., 2000. *The Land that Could Be: Environmentalism and Democracy in the Twenty-First Century*. Cambridge: MIT Press.

Simmons, B.A., 2000. International Law and State Behavior: Commitment and

Compliance in International Monetary Affairs. *American Political Science Review*, 94(4), pp.819–835.

Sprinz, D. & Vaahtoranta, T., 1994. The Interest-Based Explanation of International Environmental Policy. *International Organization*, 48(1), pp.77–105.

Steinberg, P.F., 2001. *Environmental Leadership in Developing Countries: Transnational Relations and Biodiversity Policy in Costa Rica and Bolivia*. Cambridge: MIT Press.

Tarrow, S., 2001. Transnational Politics: Contention and Institutions in International Politics. *Annual Review of Political Science*, 4(1), pp.1–20.

Timor-Leste Const., pt. II, tit. III, art. 61, § 1 (2002).

Underdal, A., 2010. Complexity and Challenges of Long-term Environmental Governance. *Global Environmental Change*, 20(3), pp.386–393.

Union of International Associations ed., 2012. *Yearbook of International Organizations 2012–2013*. Brussels: Brill.

Wapner, P., 1995. Politics Beyond the State: Environmental Activism and World Civic Politics. *World Politics*, 47(3), pp.311–340.

Yearly, S., 1996. *Sociology, Environmentalism, Globalization: Reinventing the Globe*. London: SAGE.

Zarsky, L., 1999. Havens, Halos and Spaghetti: Untangling the Evidence about Foreign Direct Investment and the Environment. In OECD, *Foreign Direct Investment and the Environment*. Paris: Organisation for Economic Co-operation and Development, pp.47–73. Available at: http://works.bepress.com/lyuba_zarsky/15 [Accessed December 20, 2013].

Chapter 4

The experiences of Nepal and Sri Lanka

Introduction

The global quantitative analysis presented in Chapter 3 reveals several factors affecting the likelihood that a state will entrench environmental rights in its national constitution. Although the statistical analysis was both spatially and temporally comprehensive, it certainly did not provide an exhaustive test of all potential explanations. In an effort to identify additional factors not captured by the quantitative portion of this study then, I proceed with the second stage of the nested analysis described earlier. In this phase, the results of the statistical analysis are used to select case studies that I subject to in-depth qualitative assessment. This approach seeks to broaden the universe of possible explanations for the presence or absence of constitutional environmental rights.

The case selection process follows a most similar systems design, which Hirschl (2005) identifies as a best practice in the application of inference-oriented methods to the study of comparative constitutional law. The process involved identifying two countries that feature similar values on the statistically significant independent variables, but different outcomes on the dependent variable (e.g., whether or not a constitutional environmental right was adopted). The specific method utilized for identifying cases is recounted below:

1 I computed the mean scores for each significant independent variable for all country-years in the data set.
2 I sorted each country-year according to whether the value for each independent variable fell above or below the mean value for that variable.[1]
3 I located countries that adopted constitutional environmental rights and searched for potential comparison countries that matched the binary value on each of the independent variables, but which have not ratified a constitution featuring an environmental right.
4 I compared the values of the independent variables during the most recent year in which a constitutional event[2] occurred.

This procedure led to the identification of two countries, Nepal and Sri Lanka,[3] that shared similar values (e.g., above or below the mean for all countries) on the independent variables during years in which constitutional events occurred,[4] but obtained different outcomes on the dependent variable (see Table 4.1).[5]

Drawing upon history, primary and secondary sources, and interviews, the remainder of this chapter discusses the unique paths that environmental rights have tread in the cases of Nepal and Sri Lanka.

Nepal: "expecting the elephant but getting the mouse"

In order to understand how the Nepali people came to adopt constitutional environmental rights, it is essential first to provide some background information and historical context. Situated in South Asia between emerging world powers China to the north and India to the south and west, Nepal is a relatively small country with a population of nearly 29 million people (World Bank 2016a). Yet, the country features significant ethnic diversity, as it houses "101 caste/ethnic groups, 91 linguistic groups and 9 religious groups" (Hachhethu et al. 2008, p.3).[6] It is one of the poorest countries in the world, as evidenced by its GDP per capita (2015) of only $732 (World Bank 2016c). In terms of human development, Nepal ranks 145th out of 188 countries (UNDP 2015). The country's infrastructure is in poor condition, the byzantine regulatory environment constrains opportunities for private sector development, and vulnerability to climate change and natural disasters remains high (World Bank 2015). However, despite its small size and low-income status, Nepal commands a wealth of biological resources (e.g., forests, plains, and the Himalayas) that, if managed in a sustainable manner, could present substantial opportunities for economic development (Oli 1996).[7]

For most of its history, Nepal existed under monarchical rule. After a brief flirtation with a multi-party system achieved through the adoption of a democratic constitution in 1959, Nepal reverted to monarchical rule in 1960 when King Mahendra seized power and installed a partyless system of governance known as the *Panchayat* regime. This system would remain in

Table 4.1 Most similar systems design for case selection

	Civil Liberties Protection	*GDP per capita*	*Int'l Civil Society Influence*	*Level of Democracy*	*Population Density*	*Constitutional Environmental Right*
Nepal	↑	↓	↓	↑	↑	**Yes**
Sri Lanka	↑	↓	↓	↑	↑	**No**

place until the first People's Movement (Jana Andolan I) occurred in 1990, and a new constitution, which "represented a dramatic advance in the evolution of a democratic, constitutional order in Nepal" (Hutt 1991, p.1039) was adopted. However, some observers criticized the document for failing to incorporate the views of traditionally marginalized groups (UNDP 2007, p.3).

Meanwhile, although this popular movement restored multiparty democracy (at least temporarily), other issues loomed around the corner. In 1996, as a result of lingering discontent about the state of social and economic inequality in Nepal (Shrestha 2007, p.2), Maoist insurgents (members of the Communist Party of Nepal-Maoist) waged an "armed struggle against the state" (Wickeri 2010, pp.427–428) or "People's War" that led to over 13,000 deaths (Tiwari 2007, p.4). This conflict exacerbated tensions in the country and increased the propensity of the state to resort to aggressive tactics to quell unrest (Kumar 2005, p.68). Royal coups in 2002 and 2005 led by King Gyanendra returned the country to the rule of the crown. Yet, the insurgency would soon come to an end and the monarchy found itself in a precarious situation when the Maoists joined forces with political parties to oppose the king. This political union coincided with the 2006 People's Movement (Jana Andolan II) in which the citizens of Nepal "[took] to the streets" to "[rally] for republicanism" and overthrow the monarchy once and for all (Hachhethu et al. 2008, p.2). It was in the wake of these events that Nepal sought to write a new, more inclusive, more democratic constitution.

While it may not be surprising to note that the process of drafting a constitution is a highly complex procedure involving multiple stakeholders, motivations, and rounds of decision-making, the analysis reported here reveals that an environmental right found its way into Nepal's 2007 Interim Constitution by more than mere constitutional borrowing (e.g., Osiatynski 2003) or policy convergence (e.g., Knill 2005). The genesis of Nepal's constitutional environmental right may best be understood as the product of contextual factors and political dynamics present prior to and during the constitution drafting process. In the space below, I develop these concepts and explain how they contributed to the phenomenon at the heart of this study.

Field research overview

In order to understand the factors that led to the promulgation of an environmental right in Nepal's 2007 Interim Constitution, I traveled to Kathmandu, Nepal during the summer of 2012.[8] From September 15 to 23, 2012, I conducted semi-structured interviews with individuals who played a variety of roles in the development of the Interim Constitution, especially where environmental issues were concerned. Some lobbied government officials while others contributed to reports presented before decision-makers at subcommittee meetings. However, only one of the interviewees actually served as a decision-maker during that process, a fact that limits the generalizability of the inferences that can be drawn from this analysis. Where possible, interview data were supplemented with literature and relevant case law. In total, I recorded over six hours of interviews with eight adult males who worked in fields such as advocacy, journalism, politics, and public interest law.

Analysis

Contextual factors

Three types of contextual factors—historical events, ongoing issues, and international influence—appear to have influenced the constitution drafting process in non-trivial ways. First, interviewees suggested that four *historical events* shaped the political environment in which the constitution was ultimately written. At the conclusion of the 1990 People's Movement and with the passage of the 1990 Constitution, the Nepalese people were granted the opportunity to establish civil society organizations, which resulted in the founding of groups that focused on addressing environmental issues. As civil society began to flourish, groups engaged in research and advocacy activities that drew attention to these concerns. For the first time, Nepalese people participated in public debates about pressing environmental problems. Thus, the environmental movement in Nepal had begun in earnest. However, ending monarchical rule, not addressing environmental problems, had been the main focus of the Movement.

Yet, the conclusion of the 1990 People's Movement quickly transitioned into a period of Maoist Conflict, which lasted for 16 years. The Conflict perturbed the popular psyche, heightening the desire to install a form of government in which people could exercise their ability to voice their concerns about the way the country was being governed. It caused people to raise their expectations regarding how responsive government should be to their concerns. As a consequence, the populace sought to replace the 1990 Constitution, play a more decisive role in the drafting of a successor document, and expand the number of rights formally recognized by the state.

The Maoist Conflict ended with another popular uprising, the 2006 People's Movement. This event signaled the end of monarchical rule in Nepal, and prompted the transition from a highly centralized form of government to a more decentralized system. Although changing the system of governance was the main focus of the Movement, it was also driven by an array of cultural, environmental, and social factors as well, which the public sought to address in a new constitution. At this point, civil society organizations, which had been in existence for over a decade, exerted their influence on the political process by actively participating in the Movement. In particular, environmental groups lobbied elected officials to include environmental rights in the new constitution. Unlike the 1990 People's Movement, which was mainly concerned with and influenced by domestic concerns,[9] the 2006 People's Movement was informed by non-governmental organizations (NGOs) that tapped into the larger global discourse on human rights. Therefore, the evidence suggests that the emergence of civil society organizations after 1990 led to the Nepalese people being exposed to ideas and concepts that broadened their scope of aspirations and demands to be placed on the new government.

In between the two People's Movements, the landmark *Godavari Marble*[10] case was decided by the Supreme Court of Nepal. The decision, delivered by Justice Laxman Prasad Aryal, held that the right to life guaranteed under Article 12(1) of the 1990 Constitution of the Kingdom of Nepal included the right to a healthy environment. While this judgment remains notable for marking the first time that the right to a healthy environment was recognized under Nepali law, it is the path that led to this creative judicial interpretation that is most relevant to the task at hand. Mr. Prakash Mani Sharma, one of the two lawyers representing the petitioners in *Godavari Marble*, studied for his Masters of Law at Delhi, where he learned of renowned Indian environmental lawyer, M.C. Mehta.[11] Inspired by M.C. Mehta's notion that the substantive right to life included the right to a healthy environment, Sharma borrowed the idea and employed it in his arguments before the Nepalese Supreme Court (Interview with P. Sharma 2012).

Writing on behalf of the Supreme Court, Justice Aryal appeared persuaded by Sharma's environmental extension of the right to life pioneered by M.C. Mehta:

> Mr. Prakash Mani Sharma and Mr. Upendra Dev Acharya, the learned Advocates, appearing on behalf of the petitioner have put forward the Article 11 (1) of the Constitution of Nepal, 2019 B.S. which provides that no person shall be deprived of his life and personal liberty save is [sic] accordance with law. The works carried out by the respondent Godawari Marble Industries have been disbalanced to the environment. The dust and sand produced during the explosions which is being undertaken in the mining process has polluted the atmosphere and water of the area and caused deforestation. Due to the continuing environmental degradation and pollution created by the said industry, Right to Life of the people has been violated. The absence of appropriate environment caused diminution of human life.[12]

Godavari Marble went on to become a fundamental legal precedent in Nepali jurisprudence (Interview with P. Sharma 2012).

The second type of contextual factor present in the Nepali case involved *ongoing issues* related to environmental conditions, governance, and the marginalization of certain ethnic groups. In terms of environmental conditions, a history of unchecked environmental degradation and deforestation dating back to at least the 1970s resulted in massive flooding and water pollution, which raised public consciousness about environmental issues. This caused the public to demand that the government address problems with environmental quality through the implementation of law and policy, specifically by including some kind of environmental provision in the constitution. One interviewee suggested that there exists a strong causal relationship between the quality of the environment and the public demand for constitutionalizing environmental protection:

> Previously [a constitutional environmental provision] was not incorporated as a right because that was not [a] problem in Nepal. Now there is organization. There is environmental degradation. There [are] too many disturbances in the climate right now that people are aware of. The Nepalese government signed so many international covenants ... When [people's] awareness level is increased ... they contact the government to [adopt an] environment right.
>
> (Interview with A. Pokharel 2012)

The heightened awareness regarding deteriorating environmental conditions spurred increased organization among members of civil society, who formed groups to advocate for changes in environmental governance.

The next set of concerns—federalism, good governance, and natural resource management—all pertained to aspects of governance in Nepal. The issue of federalism—that is, the distribution of political authority among federal, state, district, and local levels of governance—loomed large among members of civil society in the years leading up to the drafting of the Interim Constitution. Here the debate focused on identifying the proper level of governmental authority responsible for addressing certain types of environmental concerns. In particular, the Nepali people hoped to clarify the scope of environmental issues that mandated federal (as opposed to district or local) action (Interview with S. Ghimire 2012). The inability to establish a politically and environmentally responsive jurisdictional basis for addressing environmental problems with input from those who have been most affected by the existing arrangement weighed heavily in the minds of individuals acting outside the traditional corridors of power. As such, the disparity between expectations held by the public and resulting environmental outcomes seemed to suggest the need to pursue a debate on the issue. The drafting of the Interim Constitution presented such an opportunity.

Related to the structure of the government is the question of its performance in terms of practicing good governance, defined here as governance that adheres to "the rule of law, curbing corruption, and democratic accountability" (Licht et al. 2007, p.660).[13] Although environmental problems appear to have been a major concern among the Nepalese people prior to the enactment of the Interim Constitution, they also recognized that without a responsive government capable of protecting basic human rights, efforts to improve environmental quality might prove futile (Interview with G. Pandey 2012). Thus, the quest to improve the environment was viewed, at least by some, as inextricably linked to the promotion of better governance more generally. However, some Nepalese were under the impression that including an environmental right in the constitution would compel the government to enact legislation in support of achieving the stated objective.[14]

A final attribute of governance expressed during the interviews was natural resource management. In particular, prior to the adoption of the Interim Constitution, Nepalese society engaged in a serious debate over whether natural resources (e.g., forests) should be managed by the federal government, private sector, or local communities. As one respondent remarked, the legacy of natural resource mismanagement by both governmental and private actors exacerbated inequality within the country (Interview with B. Pokharel 2012). Despite the presentation of scientific evidence demonstrating that local communities, employing a collective approach to managing property, are more effective stewards of natural resources than either the government or private entities, the information fell on deaf ears in the Parliament. Only state or private property would be considered for inclusion in the new constitution, while collective property and its accompanying notion of collective rights would be off the table. Furthermore, without providing the people of Nepal with the "bundle" of requisite rights—that is, rights, responsibilities, roles, and risks—the desire for more sustainable management of natural resources would go unfulfilled (Interview with B. Pokharel 2012). Therefore, the evidence suggests that the Nepalese people had wanted greater autonomy to manage natural resources at the level of local communities, but due to considerable opposition from the government such demands went unheeded, and a much broader, more ambiguous, right was ultimately entrenched in the Interim Constitution instead.

The last ongoing issue that influenced the political climate in the time leading up to the drafting of the Interim Constitution involved the treatment of marginalized groups. Traditionally, groups such as Dalits, Janajatis, people in rural areas, the poor, and women were prevented from becoming upwardly mobile in Nepalese society by the elite and upper castes, who restricted their access to land and other natural resources (Interview with N.S. Paudel 2012). Following the boom in the establishment of NGOs after 1990, members of civil society actively sought to improve the prospects for social equality among Nepal's most vulnerable populations, who had suffered ills such as food scarcity at the hands of an neglectful central government (Upreti et al. 2010). One strategy proposed to address this problem centered on strengthening legal rights for marginalized groups, specifically where access to land and resources were implicated. Drawing inspiration from the discourse surrounding minority rights, this approach sought not only to provide corrective justice for vulnerable peoples but also to advance the demand for gaining local ownership over environmental resources (Interview with N.S. Paudel 2012). However, as the discussion of natural resource management above suggests, this problem would fail to be addressed in the manner desired by both civil society and the marginalized groups, as land rights remained curiously absent from the new constitution, while a very general environmental right wound up being included instead.

The third type of contextual factor was *international influence*. First, members of civil society in Nepal were cognizant of provisions relating to environmental rights appearing in or interpreted by courts to be found in the constitutions of other countries around the world. In particular, the constitutions of Bolivia, Ecuador, India, and Namibia were cited as authoritative exemplars that were used to bolster the argument for including environmental rights in Nepal's Interim Constitution during advocacy efforts and government consultations (Interviews with D. Khanal 2012 and P. Sharma 2012).

Second, as stated earlier, knowledge of relevant foreign jurisprudence, specifically India's series of cases brought by M.C. Mehta, influenced the types of arguments made by legal counsel in *Godavari Marble*, which not only established a legal precedent for the constitutional protection of environmental rights, but also sensitized judges to the concept of environmental rights. Some of these judges would later take part in the drafting of the Interim Constitution. Interestingly, Justice Laxman Prasad Aryal, the Supreme Court justice who delivered the opinion in *Godavari Marble*, became the chair of the Interim Constitution Drafting Committee (ICDC), which was charged with making the final decisions about the content of the Interim Constitution.[15]

Finally, international law may have played a small but significant role in shaping the context in which the Interim Constitution was written. Interviewees spoke in general of the importance of international covenants to which Nepal was a party and in particular about the International Labor Organization Convention No. 169 concerning Indigenous and Tribal Peoples in Independent Countries (ILO 169), which seeks to promote the rights of such peoples (ILO 1989). While Nepal did not officially ratify ILO 169 until after the adoption of the Interim Constitution, one respondent indicated that this legally binding international document "contributed to the inclusion of environment" in the Interim Constitution (Interview with P. Sharma 2012). In short, although the direct causal linkages are not firmly established, international influences such as foreign constitutions, foreign jurisprudence, and international law may have contributed to the overall political environment that facilitated public discourse on the topic of environmental rights and informed the advocacy efforts of civil society actors who sought to influence the agenda of decision-making bodies charged with drafting the Interim Constitution.

Political dynamics

During the process of drafting the Interim Constitution, certain political dynamics helped to shape discussions among decision-makers and stakeholders, and influenced the kind of content that ultimately became entrenched in the document. An analysis of the interviews resulted in the identification of three generic categories or types of political dynamics—actions, controversies, and political environment.

First, the constitution drafting process in Nepal was impacted by *actions*, which I define as "deliberate acts undertaken by people inside or outside government to have environmental issues formally addressed." In particular, three subcategories of actions were identified—advocacy, collaboration, and support. The type of action most commonly cited by interviewees was advocacy, which concerned the pro-environmental lobbying efforts of individuals and organizations in Nepal's civil society. Advocacy consisted of two kinds of activities—(1) when civil society actors attempted to shape the content of the constitution by interfacing directly with members of constitution drafting subcommittees either through presentations or providing written commentary to the subcommittees,[16] and (2) when civil society actors attempted to shape the content of the constitution by interacting with others who presented before the constitution drafting subcommittees.[17] There were multiple opportunities for civil society to voice their concerns both directly and indirectly, although final decisions regarding the language of content related to the environment were made first by subcommittees[18] and then the superior committee, the ICDC, before the document as a whole was put to a vote in the Constituent Assembly.

Collaboration, or "acts in which different sectors of society banded together to advocate for changes in environmental policy," also took place during the drafting process. This form of action was manifested in the establishment of the Natural Resource People's Parliament (NRPP)—a network of actors cutting across different sectors of Nepali society, united by the desire to leverage varying connections and capacities to influence the direction of environmental governance in Nepal. As one interviewee explained, this group served as both a sounding board and popular decision-making body that sought to represent the interests of the Nepali people by providing constitution drafting entities with intellectual input (Interview with B. Pokharel 2012). The NRPP worked in concert with domestic and international NGOs such as the International Union for Conservation of Nature (IUCN-Nepal) and the Federation of Community Forestry Users, Nepal (FECOFUN) to influence the political parties (which selected the individuals who staffed the committees and subcommittees vested with decision-making authority), subcommittees, ICDC, and Parliament (Interview with A. Pokharel 2012).

Another form of action noted during the interviews was support, or "acts involving members of government who actively lobbied for or did not oppose the inclusion of environmental rights in the Interim Constitution." In particular, respondents singled out political parties as the main governmental actors who sought to include an environmental rights provision in the new constitution. Interestingly, two interviewees suggested that environmental rights were not subject to controversy among members of relevant subcommittees that entertained the idea. According to these respondents, there was no debate over the decision to include environmental rights and no one objected to their adoption (Interviews with D. Khanal 2012 and G. Pandey 2012). However, as detailed in the above section on natural resource management, there was an apparent gap between the environmental rights provision put forth by the subcommittees and the kind of language pertaining to environmental rights accepted by the ICDC. Ultimately, the Interim Constitution did not include an environmental right dealing with the right of local communities to manage natural resources. Although less is known about the internal discussions carried out within the ICDC, it stands to reason that this decision-making entity is responsible for amending the content of the environmental rights provision. Not surprisingly, this result was greeted with frustration by members of civil society (Interview with B. Pokharel 2012).

Second, the constitution drafting process was motivated by major societal *controversies*. The concept of environmental rights seemed relatively unproblematic, at least within committees subordinate to the ICDC. However, two other, albeit related, topics generated considerable differences of opinion. First, the continuing state of economic and social inequality intimately tied to access to land was a major driving factor behind the desire to adopt natural resource property rights in the new constitution. With the memory of undemocratic state behavior regarding land ownership still fresh in the minds of the public, people sought to develop restrictions that would ensure the government would not revert to land expropriation in the future. However, the state seemed reluctant to accept the institutionalization of collective property rights, fearing that it would upset the existing legal order in which only private and state property rights were recognized (Interview with B. Pokharel 2012). Second, the country's long history of monarchical rule and violent efforts to install a system of government responsive to the demands of the people necessitated a direct and public discussion of power sharing arrangements.

The discourse fell mainly along ideological lines, with the left-wing Maoists favoring a strong central government and the right-wing Nepali Congregation promoting individual rights. More generally, the debate over power sharing dealt with deciding the distribution of authority among government leaders (e.g., Parliament and president, president and prime minister) and among levels of governance (e.g., federal and local) (Interviews with D. Khanal 2012 and B. Pokharel 2012). The interviewees asserted that natural resource property rights and power sharing, not environmental rights, figured most prominently as issues to be addressed during the constitution drafting process.

Third, attributes of the *political environment* during the time in which the Interim Constitution was drafted likely played a role in determining the language that was finally adopted.[19] Not only were the Nepalese people at the time aware of environmental degradation and climate-related issues in the country, but also political parties were aware that people wanted the concept of environmental justice addressed in the new constitution.[20] In light of the 2006 People's Movement that immediately preceded the drafting of the Interim Constitution, the Nepalese people elevated their expectations in terms of what they believed the new constitution would do to improve their ability to voice their concerns and have the government attend to them. More precisely, the public felt that they would be granted more rights and improved recognition of those rights. The political parties fed these expectations by assuring the people that the "constitution is the main thing that will save everything" (Interview with B. Pokharel 2012). Members of the legal and human rights activist communities also shared a strategic interest in promoting the adoption of constitutional environmental rights. These groups argued that the existing legal infrastructure in its current format was incapable of providing environmental justice. In order to enhance the prospects for Nepalese citizens to obtain environmental justice, environmental rights would need to be instantiated in the constitution (Interview with D. Khanal 2012). In addition, historical events and recognition of the importance of this particular constitutional moment constituted a sense of opportunity. The two People's Movements brought different kinds of opportunity; the 1990 People's Movement created a space for civil society organizations in Nepal, while the 2006 People's Movement introduced the country to a more comprehensive human rights discourse (Interview with N.S. Paudel 2012).

The range of actors involved in the constitution drafting process, in addition to the roles in which they served, were arguably the most important aspects of the political environment. Unlike the 1990 Constitution, for which the king nominated those who would become the architects of the charter, the drafting of the Interim Constitution involved a more inclusive process whereby the people could express their opinions through elected representatives in Parliament and civil society organizations. This change was a function of both the reduced role of the monarchy as well as the political space created for civil society (Interview with B. Pokharel 2012). Turnover in the Constituent Assembly also reinvigorated the institution with a younger, more globally conscious generation of legislators (Interview with P. Sharma 2012). Finally, it was of no small consequence that Hon. Laxman Prasad Aryal, a justice whose amenability to the concept of environmental rights was clearly articulated in *Godavari Marble*, served as the chair of the ICDC, the most powerful committee in the constitution drafting process (Interview with P.M. Sharma 2012). When viewed in concert, these aspects of the political environment present a compelling suite of temporally bound conditions that may have contributed significantly to the adoption of a constitutional environmental right in the Interim Constitution.

Discussion

The results of the qualitative content analysis highlight several factors that contributed to the enactment of a constitutional environmental right in Nepal. Historically, the 1990 People's Movement appears to have been indispensable in explaining the phenomenon observed. This Movement was responsible for creating the political space required for civil society to blossom. Civil society organizations went on to raise awareness about human rights and environmental issues and advocate on behalf of the Nepalese people. To be sure, the 2006 People's Movement exposed Nepal to a broader human rights discourse and elevated the level of demands that Nepalese citizens placed on their government. However, these aspects of the latter movement could have been effectively checked by a recalcitrant authority and thus rendered impotent. Therefore, at least in part, the adoption of a constitutional environmental right in Nepal may be said to have been enabled by both an historical contingency[21] and a major alteration to the political opportunity structure.

At the same time, critical junctures and opportunity structures are influenced by the context in which they exist. In the case of Nepal, the main contextual factor that served as the impetus to enact substantial environmental policy reform at the constitutional level was environmental degradation, mainly as a result of deforestation (Gilmour 1988). Thus, poor environmental quality, the product of increasing industrialization, precipitated the need for enhanced legal protection. Without a damaged environment that negatively impacted the lives of Nepalese citizens, it is unlikely that the desire for constitutional action on environmental issues would have developed.

Sri Lanka: a rose by any other name?

An island located off the southeastern coast of India, Sri Lanka has a population of just more than 20 million people and a GDP per capita (2015) of $3,912 (World Bank 2016b). Its human development score ranks 73rd out of 188 countries and 91 percent of the adult population is literate (UNDP 2015). Following the conclusion of an internal conflict that lasted 26 years and ended in May 2009, Sri Lanka has experienced strong economic growth and a concomitant decline in poverty. However, despite a decade of sustained economic advancement, several areas throughout the country remain mired in moderate levels of impoverishment (World Bank 2016b). Sri Lanka made substantial progress towards achieving many of its MDGs, such as eradicating extreme poverty and hunger and achieving universal primary education, although persistent challenges remain in combating infectious diseases and ensuring environmental sustainability (UN, Sri Lanka 2015).

Sri Lanka's history is punctuated by alternating periods of concurrent kingdoms and unification, colonial control, and, up until recently, civil conflict. In the space that follows I will focus on aspects of Sri Lankan constitutional history from the 1500s onwards. During the 16th century, Sri Lanka consisted of three kingdoms: "the Tamil kingdom of Jaffna in the north, the Kotte kingdom with its capital in Colombo, and the kingdom of Kandy in the central highlands" (Hill 2008, p.142). The geographic and political division among the kingdoms enabled successive colonizers to achieve dominion over the island, which bestowed upon Sri Lanka "the longest history of colonialism in South Asia" (Rajepakse 2008, p.1). With the aid of strong naval forces, the Portuguese sought to conquer the three kingdoms but were only successful in subjugating Jaffna and Kotte. European continental disputes spilled over into Sri Lanka, and by 1658 the Dutch effectively expelled the Portuguese from the country. The Dutch initially concentrated their efforts on weakening the formidable Kandyan kingdom, but this approach was unsupported by the leadership back in Holland, who preferred to maintain a focus on maximizing resource exploitation for commercial gain. Meanwhile, Dutch dominance was undermined by the English East India Company's geopolitical interest in access to Kandyan ports. Eventually, the British capitalized upon the diminished position of the Dutch in the wake of the French Revolution and seized control of Dutch possessions in Sri Lanka in 1795–1796. Sri Lanka, or Ceylon as it was known at the time, formally became a British Crown Colony in January 1802 (de Silva 1981).

The British established complete sovereignty over the country by 1818, ushering in an extended period of successive constitutional reforms. The Colebrooke–Cameron reforms of 1833 recommended, *inter alia*, consolidating provinces into a single administrative unit, establishing representative legislative bodies, and creating an independent judicial system. Many of the reforms were implemented, and a new constitution offering some adjustments to the system of representation was promulgated in 1910. However, the growing tension between the English-speaking elite class and the broader public instigated calls for a new wave of reforms. The Special Commission on the Constitution, led by Earl Donoughmore, suggested the introduction of universal suffrage, geographic representation, and executive committees focused on ministerial subjects. Although the Donoughmore Constitution was never fully implemented and only lasted 16 years, it paved the way for a relatively peaceful transition to independence. Following the passage of the Ceylon Independence Act of 1947, Ceylon became an independent member of the British Commonwealth. In 1948, the terse Soulbury Constitution, intended to install the Westminster model of governance, came into effect. With the inclusion of Article 29(2), which offered protection for the free exercise of religion, human rights became formally codified in the country's constitutional law (Rajepakse 2008).

In 1972, Sri Lanka, as the former colony was now called, adopted a new constitution that asserted its status as an independent republic and articulated directives and human rights in the form of chapters entitled "Principles of State Policy" and "Fundamental Rights and Freedoms," respectively. Significantly, the latter chapter included a provision guaranteeing Sri Lankans the right to life under Article 18(1)(b). In 1977, the ruling regime responsible for crafting the 1972 constitution suffered major electoral defeats. The new government, led by the United National Party, endeavored to amend the existing charter but ultimately decided to enact an entirely new constitution. Notably, both chapters on "Principles of State Policy" and "Fundamental Rights and Freedoms" underwent important revisions, including the addition of environmental directives in the former and the elimination of the right to life in the latter. It is this constitution, along with its 18 subsequent amendments, that currently provides the architecture for governance in Sri Lanka.[22]

Field research overview

In order to understand why constitutional environmental rights have not been adopted in Sri Lanka, I traveled to Colombo, Sri Lanka during the spring of 2013.[23] From March 27 to April 1, 2013, I conducted semi-structured interviews with individuals who possessed knowledge of Sri Lankan law and/or politics. In total, I completed over two and a half hours of interviews with five adult males and two adult females who worked in fields such as diplomacy, government administration, law, policy, and research.

Attempting to decipher the reason why a particular event did not happen presents certain methodological difficulties. I was unable to interview anyone who participated directly in the drafting of the 1978 Constitution, and I only interviewed one person who played an important role in proposing new fundamental rights for the 2000 Draft Constitution. In many cases, interviewees provided subjective speculations regarding the topic of interest. Therefore, this section offers only tentative explanations for the absence of constitutional environmental rights in Sri Lanka, based on information drawn from interviews and augmented by scholarly literature and case law. The results of my analysis reveal that the reasons why environmental rights were not incorporated into either the 1978 Constitution or the 2000 Draft Constitution differ significantly between the constitutional events, but may be construed as mainly relating to domestic political dynamics. In the case of the former, the exclusion of environmental rights was not deliberate; instead, the drafters focused on legalizing civil and political rights. In the case of the latter, the omission was likely to have been the product of several factors that affected the demand for such rights and the ability of government to address concerns about environmental quality in the country. I develop these explanations further below.

Analysis

1978 Constitution

Interview data suggest that environmental rights did not appear in the 1978 Constitution for at least two reasons. First, the environment was not a central concern during the drafting of this constitution (Interview with S. Pilapitiya 2013). On the contrary, the United National Party, which enjoyed an overwhelming majority in Parliament following the 1977 elections and was led by Prime Minister Junius Richard (J.R.) Jayewardane, "was animated by two concerns—the need for political stability and the need for rapid modernization" (Coomaraswamy 1984, p.40). Political stability involved addressing questions regarding the participation of the Tamils in democratic processes. The desire to achieve rapid modernization was inspired by the economic and industrial successes observed in Singapore and South Korea. Second, the Sri Lankan government emphasized the protection of civil and political rights in the constitution rather than social and economic rights (Interview with J. Wickramaratne 2013).[24] Moreover, the government responsible for drafting the constitution was right-wing and would not allow "the restriction of civil and political rights in the interests of principles of a social and economic nature" (Wickramaratne 1996, p.27). These conditions resulted in a new constitution that privileged first-generation human rights.

The literature suggests additional explanations for the particular content featured in the 1978 Constitution. First, the chapter on "Fundamental Rights," the section of a constitution in which one might find a provision on environmental rights, was drafted by law-makers who were influenced by the Constitution of the Fifth Republic of France (de Silva 1979, p.193), the American Bill of Rights, the "Fundamental Rights" chapter of the Indian Constitution, and the UDHR (Sharvananda 1993, pp.13–14).[25] As none of these documents contains environmental rights, it is not surprising that this particular intellectual derivative is similarly devoid of such provisions. Second, while the 1978 Constitution presented numerous changes from its predecessor,[26] it was not intended "to be ideologically innovative"; instead, it was crafted with the aim of addressing "immediate economic and social problems" (Coomaraswamy 1984, pp.54–55). The fact that environmental rights were not incorporated into the document may be, therefore, a logical outgrowth of constitutional pragmatism or perhaps a signal that environmental issues were considered to be neither immediate, nor economic/social, nor problematic at the time. Third, the government, in the form of the Select Committee on the Revision of the Constitution, did in fact solicit the advice of the general public on which fundamental rights to include in the 1978 Constitution through a questionnaire that was published in major newspapers.[27]

Post-1978–2000 Draft Constitution

Following the ratification of the 1978 Constitution, an unsuccessful attempt was made to enact a new constitution in 2000. Like its forebear, the 2000 Draft Constitution did not include environmental rights. However, the absence of environmental rights in this contemporary document can be explained as the product of four conditions—actions, controversies, political environment, and process—that informed the political dynamics in Sri Lanka on this subject for at least two decades.

First, *actions* taken or not taken by civil society or government affected the prospect of adopting environmental rights in the 2000 Draft Constitution. While it was suggested during one interview that "there hasn't been a strong environmental lobby" (Interview with M. Gomez 2013) to advocate for the inclusion of a right to the environment in this draft,[28] civil society groups did in fact urge the Parliamentary Select Committee on the Constitution to consider adding a right to a clean environment. However, these groups were unsuccessful in convincing law-makers of the importance of this provision, as "none of the drafts put forward by the government made any reference to environmental rights" (Atapattu 2001, p.293). With regard to the government, the general attitude of the leadership has been to relegate environmental rights to the realm of "luxuries that can be postponed" until Sri Lankans "solve other pressing problems of the present" (Interview with R. Algama 2013). However, this does not mean that government actors have not endeavored to promulgate constitutional environmental rights. Indeed, formal legal recognition of such rights has been attempted at least three times since 1978[29]—in the 1995 draft of the National Environmental Act, in the 1997 Government's Proposals for Constitutional Reform, and in the 2008 Draft Constitutional Bill of Rights. Yet, none of these documents ultimately became law and thus constitutional environmental rights in Sri Lanka remain absent from the legal infrastructure. A discussion of the 1997 Government's Proposals for Constitutional Reform and the 2008 Draft Constitutional Bill of Rights follows.

Following the distribution of the March 1997 draft of the government's proposed constitution, the Law & Society Trust, a Sri Lankan legal research and advocacy organization, assembled a group of experts and activists to review the document and make recommendations to the Parliamentary Select Committee on the Constitution (Atapattu 1998, p.182). The Working Group published their recommendations in a lobby document shortly thereafter. Some of the Group's suggestions were incorporated in the October 1997 draft of the proposed constitution, but the request to include the right to a clean and healthy environment went unheeded. However, certain provisions relating to environmental rights did make it into the October edition. In Chapter III ("Fundamental Rights and Freedoms"), Article 8(1) guarantees the right to life and Article 21(1) provides a right to ownership of property "subject to the preservation and protection of the environment and the rights of the community" (Government of Sri Lanka 1997, p.287). In Chapter VI ("Principles of State Policy and Fundamental Duties"), under the section on "Principles of State Policy," Article 53(6) stipulates that "[t]he State shall protect and preserve and improve the environment and safeguard the reefs, shores, forests, lakes, watercourses and wildlife of Sri Lanka" (Government of Sri Lanka 1997, p.295). Finally, the "Fundamental Duties" section of the same chapter mandates under Article 54(6) that "[i]t shall be the duty of every citizen to ... protect and improve the environment and conserve its riches" (Government of Sri Lanka 1997, p.296). All of these proposed provisions were included in the 2000 Constitution Bill using the same phrasing as that which appears in the October 1997 draft, with the exception of the fundamental duty relating to the environment, which added the phrase "and value all forms of life."

The Draft Bill of Rights includes a "Right to an Adequate Environment" under Section 14T: "All persons have the right to an environment that is—(a) not harmful to their health or well being; and (b) protected for the benefit of present and future generations" (Wickramaratne et al. 2009).[30] While the Draft Constitutional Bill of Rights did receive mention in the 2011 National Action Plan for the Protection and Promotion of Human Rights (although environmental rights were not specifically addressed), the document can only be considered to have afforded the Bill of Rights tacit, tentative endorsement rather than granting full legal effect:

> The commitment of the Government of Sri Lanka towards the full realization and guaranteeing of Human Rights was further manifested when in 2008, a Committee was appointed to give effect to proposals in Mahinda Chinthana [President Mahinda Rajapakse's national development policy framework], for the inclusion of a comprehensive Bill of the Rights into the Constitution. A Draft Bill of Rights was thereafter formulated which is being deliberated by stakeholders, *with a view to its incorporation.*
>
> (Sri Lanka Ministry of Plantation Industries and Office of Special Envoy on Human Rights 2011, p.9; emphasis added)

Second, *controversies*, or central political debates that occurred before and during the constitutional reform process, focused drafting efforts and political negotiations on addressing topics other than constitutional environmental rights. Interviewees identified devolution of power as the main focal point of the deliberations (Interview M. Gomez 2013). Here, the concern revolved around ethnic power sharing and striking an appropriate balance of power between the varying levels of governance in Sri Lanka. As with the drafting processes in 1972 and 1978, environmental concerns did not feature prominently in the preparation of the 2000 Draft Constitution.

Third, and perhaps most importantly, the *political environment*, that is, contextual and institutional factors present during the constitution drafting or reform process that may have informed decisions about whether and how to address environmental issues in the constitution, appears to have had a discernible impact on the likelihood of including environmental rights in the Sri Lankan constitution. Three such factors were determined to have influenced the level of interest in pursuing constitutional environmental rights—consciousness, judicial receptiveness, and the legal framework. In the years immediately following ratification of the 1978 Constitution, rights consciousness in general was said to be noticeably undeveloped in the country. One observer argues that this lacuna has been the result of a "lack of legal discourse or doctrine in Anglo-American constitutionalism which adequately deal with the dilemmas of development," which stifled the creation of innovative legal doctrine and established a culture of judicial deference to the executive branch (Coomaraswamy 1984, p.74).

These institutional conditions were compounded by the absence of groups that advocated taking a rights-based approach to redressing grievances. Although it is by no means a direct measure of increasing consciousness, from the time of Sri Lanka's independence in 1948 until the middle of 1972 only seven ENGOs operated in the country. Following the United Nations Conference on the Human Environment in 1972 until the middle of 1992, 176 ENGOs were founded. From July 1992 through June 2002, advocacy efforts in this area expanded dramatically, as 468 ENGOs came into being (Wickremaratne 2004). This evidence suggests that a sizable environmental civil society has emerged in the country. In this context, one interviewee argued that the people of Sri Lanka possess an awareness of environmental issues (Interview with J. Dhanapala 2013). But general awareness does not necessarily translate to enhanced prospects for regulatory enforcement. Results from a limited survey (N = 100) of employees at small- and medium-sized enterprises in Sri Lanka indicate that while an overwhelming majority of respondents acknowledge the importance of environmental protection, awareness of specific environmental regulations remains uneven (Weerasiri & Zhengang 2012). Thus, despite the presence of an environmental civil society and growing cognizance of environmental issues, these developments apparently have not (yet) translated into a popular campaign to see environmental rights formally recognized in the constitution.

Judicial receptiveness, or the degree to which the court system has positively embraced environmental litigation brought under existing legal instruments, offers another potential explanation for the absence of constitutional environmental rights in Sri Lanka. One respondent described how "courts have been sympathetic" to public interest litigation on the environment,[31] which has enabled environmental groups to bring cases using the extant legal regime instead of focusing efforts on adding a new right to the constitution (Interview with M. Gomez 2013). Other interviewees echoed that the courts have interpreted existing statutes and constitutional provisions in ways that have resulted in favorable judgments for claimants who seek to have environmental grievances redressed (Interviews with R. Algama 2013 and R. Rajepakse 2013). Four examples from Sri Lankan case law help to support these assertions.

In *The Environmental Foundation Ltd v. Attorney-General*,[32] the Supreme Court allowed the petitioner, an ENGO, to bring a case against the government on the basis that fundamental rights had been violated.[33] The Supreme Court did not rule on the issue of *locus standi* directly, but it signaled its willingness to entertain claims made by organizations representing the public interest on environmental concerns. In *Ashik v. Bandula and Others* (*Noise Pollution Case*),[34] the Supreme Court held that noise pollution emanating from loudspeakers at a mosque constituted a violation of the fundamental right to equal protection caused by the failure of the executive to properly safeguard the public from the harmful effects of noise pollution, as mandated under the National Environmental Act.[35] This decision demonstrated that the Court was open to resolving environmental claims under the banner of fundamental rights when couched in terms of public nuisance doctrine. In the *Bulankulama v. Ministry of Industrial Development (Eppawala Phosphate Mining)*[36] case, Justice Amerasinghe, writing on behalf of the Supreme Court, determined that an agreement with a U.S. company to exploit a phosphate mine in Eppawala "should be considered in light of the principles embodied in the Stockholm Declaration on the

Human Environment of 1972 and the Rio Declaration on Environment and Development of 1992" (Voigt 2009, p.181). With its extensive reliance on international soft law, "the Court clearly endorsed principles of international environmental law, including sustainable development and stressed that development activities in Sri Lanka should be evaluated against these principles" (Atapattu 2001, p.296). Finally, in *Watte Gedara Wijebanda v. Conservator General of Forest,*[37] the Supreme Court found that the fundamental right to equal protection guaranteed under the constitution inherently includes the right to a clean environment and the principle of inter-generational equity (Karunaratne 2009, p.36). Members of the Court also relied on public trust doctrine and international laws pertaining to sustainable development to inform their interpretation of the Sri Lankan environmental legal regime. Thus, this case provided jurisprudential recognition of a constitutional environmental right through a broad interpretation of the equal protection provision. In short, where environmental issues are concerned, the Sri Lankan Supreme Court has looked to international law on sustainable development for guidance, and has liberally interpreted fundamental rights in the constitution in ways favorable to plaintiffs, perhaps eliminating the need among interested parties to enact constitutional environmental rights.

The final element of the political environment that may have lessened the desire to adopt constitutional environmental rights lies in Sri Lanka's legal framework, understood here as the presence or absence of existing legal or policy instruments that are designed to achieve pro-environmental and/or human rights outcomes.[38] In terms of Sri Lanka's environmental regulatory infrastructure, one respondent remarked how "the incorporation of [an environmental right] as a constitutional feature has never struck people as being either necessary or being important as long as it is there in the policy guidance" (Interview with J. Dhanapala 2013). To be sure, Sri Lanka has an extensive history of environmental regulation that spans over 2,000 years. Following its independence from Britain in 1948, the country adopted a new set of environmental laws and ratified several international treaties relating to the environment (Zubair 2001, p.471). By the late 1970s, it was estimated that over the past hundred years or more Sri Lanka had promulgated at least 50 laws relating to the environment (Wijayadasa 1994, p.vi). Constitutional law, codes, and statutes were cited by interviewees as contributing substantially to a robust environmental legal framework that might render constitutional environmental rights unnecessary at best and redundant at worst.[39]

In the absence of constitutional environmental rights, alternative constitutional provisions have been utilized in Sri Lanka to achieve similar ends. Interviewees specifically mentioned provisions contained within Chapter III ("Fundamental Rights") and Chapter VI ("Directive Principles of State Policy and Fundamental Duties").[40] Regarding the former, Article 12(1) of the 1978 Constitution on the right to equality,[41] has proved to be particularly useful in framing the legal claims of plaintiffs in environmental litigation, especially where human rights are implicated (Interview with R. Rajepakse 2013).[42] In addition, Article 126 allows individuals to petition the Supreme Court directly where a violation of fundamental rights is alleged, bolstering the ability to bring a claim relevant to the equality provision and thus offering a potential avenue for redressing environmental grievances. Regarding the latter, Article 27(14) in the section on "Directive Principles of State Policy" declares that "[t]he State shall protect, preserve and improve the environment for the benefit of the community" (Sri Lanka Const., art. 27, § 14 (1978)). Under the section on "Fundamental Duties," Article 28(f) states that it is the duty of every person in Sri Lanka "to protect nature and conserve its riches" (Sri Lanka Const., art. 28, § f (1978)). Considered in tandem, these provisions "have been cited as the general principles on which environmental litigation has been based" (Interview with R. Rajepakse 2013).

Sri Lankans may also seek to resolve environmental problems in court using codes and established common law doctrine relating to public and private nuisance (Interview with R. Rajepakse 2013). In the case of public nuisance, claims can be brought before local magistrates "under Section 98 of the Code of Criminal Procedure Act No. 15 of 1979, and under Section 261, 283 and 284 of the Penal Code No. 2 of 1883" (Schukoske 1996, p.158). Bringing complaints under public nuisance presents potential claimants with a viable alternative to engaging in environmental litigation before the Supreme Court on the basis of alleged fundamental rights violations. There are magistrate's courts throughout the island, but only one Supreme Court located in Colombo.[43] The public nuisance avenue affords lay people, especially those living in remote areas, greater access to courts (Interview with R. Rajepakse 2013). In addition, compared with fundamental rights litigation, "public nuisance actions are simpler, speedier, and have better remedies" (Schukoske 1996, p.168, n. 60).

Finally, certain statutes have been invoked to establish a cause of action where environmental problems have arisen, serving a function similar to that which inheres in constitutional environmental rights. In the case of environmental pollution, public nuisance provides the basis for registering complaints with either the Central Environmental Authority (CEA)[44] or the police (Interview with M. Wimalasena 2013), as stipulated by section 31 of the National Environmental Act (NEA)[45] and a 1995 circular from the Inspector General of Police, respectively.[46] Once a complaint has been made, "officers of the CEA go and inspect the industry" (Interview with M. Wimalasena 2013). If it is determined that the source has been operating without the required Environmental Protection License (EPL),[47] the file is sent to the CEA's legal division, where staff will decide whether or not to file suit in order to compel the violator to engage in pollution mitigation activities. In addition, the National Environmental Regulations No. 1 of 1993 under the NEA provide procedural environmental rights in the context of potential environmental impacts of new development projects. Under this provision, the public may participate in the EIA process.[48] Specifically, "[t]he public can participate at the 'scoping' stage, review the EIA for 30 days, request clarifications from the [project proponent] through the [project-approving agency] and may, at the discretion of the [project-approving agency], participate at a public hearing" (Zubair 2001, p.473).[49]

Fourth, *process*, or "the internal motivating factors that have shaped the nature and outcomes of constitutional reform efforts," likely played an important role in determining the content of the 2000 Draft Constitution. The main factor cited as having a major impact on the product was the degree of politicization marking the reform discussions. In particular, "[c]onstitutional reform ... has been driven really by the interests of the party in power" as opposed to a "principled, open, transparent process" (Interview with M. Gomez 2013). To be sure, politicization of constitutional reform is not a new phenomenon in Sri Lanka. Indeed, the country has a history in which "[t]he making and unmaking of constitutions seems to have now become more a matter of prestige for political parties than a serious and deliberate exercise" (Jayasuriya 1982, p.2). Previous constitutions have been criticized for "serving the government" (Coomaraswamy 1984, p.55), being "partisan" and "non-consensual" (Edrisinha 2007, p.133), and having been drafted in a "slipshod manner" (Perera 1979, p.107).

Discussion

The results of the qualitative content analysis present several explanations for the absence of constitutional environmental rights in Sri Lanka. In terms of the 1978 Constitution, had the drafting process focused on addressing environmental issues, including third-generation human rights and featuring innovative solutions to future problems, it is more likely that environmental rights would have been firmly planted in the chapter on "Fundamental Rights." During the drafting of the 1978 Constitution, lawmakers sought only to provide basic human rights that reflected contemporary international norms. At the global level, environmental rights were still in their infancy.[50] The majority of the drafting effort focused on designing political institutions.

In terms of the post-1978 era in Sri Lanka, three conditions seem to have been particularly influential. First, had the focus of constitutional reform not been consumed by the issue of devolution of power, it might have freed up political capital to address other important problems facing the developing country. Second, without substantial support from the judiciary to see that environmental grievances are redressed, Sri Lankans might have decided to pursue more constitutional solutions to problems such as pollution and environmental degradation resulting from economic development. Third, if Sri Lanka's legal framework had been undeveloped or critically lacking in the area of environmental regulation, perhaps the people of Sri Lanka, not just a single Working Group, would have made a major push to include environmental rights in the constitution.

Conclusion: synthesis and theoretical implications

The two case studies help to reveal factors not identified in the global statistical analysis of constitutional environmental rights that may be causally important in explaining the outcomes observed in Nepal and Sri Lanka. On the basis of a comparative analysis, it is possible to uncover historical and/or structural influences on decision-making regarding constitutional provisions. Moreover, this study offers insights on whether prospects for pursuing constitutional environmental protection are influenced more by factors endogenous or exogenous to the state. The results are summarized in Table 4.2.

As Table 4.2 indicates, both historical and structural factors played an important role in determining the likelihood that either country would adopt a constitutional environmental right. Interestingly, each of these factors relates primarily to conditions internal to the state and secondarily to conditions of the international environment. These findings lead to a conclusion that supplements the results of the global statistical analysis cited earlier: the likelihood that a country will adopt a constitutional environmental right is directly associated with its domestic political conditions and structures, and indirectly associated with the international normative context in which its constitution is written. Importantly, however, the results show that "domestic factors can affect the responsiveness to international policy promotion in both positive and negative directions" (Busch & Jörgens 2014, p.260).

Table 4.2 Factors that increased(+)/decreased(–) the likelihood of adopting constitutional environmental rights in Nepal (N) and Sri Lanka (SL)

	Endogenous Factors	*Exogenous Factors*
Historical Factors	1990 People's Movement (N+) Environmental degradation (N+) 1978: Stability, modernization (SL–) Post-1978: Devolution of power (SL–)	
Structural Factors	Judicial receptiveness (SL–) Legal framework (SL–)	Judicial receptiveness (SL–)

In the case of Nepal, the inclusion of an environmental right in the 2007 Interim Constitution was facilitated by two major historical factors: the 1990 People's Movement and the issue of ongoing environmental degradation. The 2007 Interim Constitution was drafted at a time when civil society groups focused on the environment and human rights had been active for over 15 years, and concerns about environmental degradation had steadily increased as the country wrestled with economic development. By 2007, approximately 69 countries had already adopted constitutional environmental rights, and jurisprudence within the region had established a link between human rights and environmental protection. These external factors conditioned the normative environment in which the 2007 Interim Constitution was written, providing a set of ideas that had gained widespread acceptance since their official inception in 1974.

Although not determined to be directly influential in the enactment of a constitutional environmental right, three types of international influences—foreign constitutions, foreign jurisprudence, and international law—indirectly affected the likelihood that Nepal would include an environmental right in its 2007 Interim Constitution. In particular, the constitutions of Bolivia, Ecuador, and Namibia, as well as Indian environmental case law and ILO 169 were all cited by interviewees as external influences that affected the decision to promulgate a constitutional environmental right. There is insufficient evidence of their intentional usage during the constitution drafting process to afford them causal importance. However, at the very least these sources of international influence may be construed as having shaped the ideational context in which the constitution was written.

In the case of Sri Lanka, the absence of environmental rights in either the 1978 Constitution or the 2000 Draft Constitution occurred as a result of two historical factors (a focus on stability and modernization present during the drafting of the former constitution, and on the devolution of power present during the time leading up to the latter constitution) and two structural factors (judicial receptiveness to redressing environmental grievances through litigation and the existence of a robust environmental legal framework). While neither the 1978 Constitution nor the 2000 Draft Constitution featured environmental rights, these results can be seen as the product of different reasoning. When the 1978 Constitution was drafted, environmental rights were in their infancy. At this point in time only two countries—Yugoslavia (1974) and Portugal (1976)—had adopted constitutional environmental rights. In addition, concerns regarding political stability and modernization, rather than the environment, dominated political discourse during the constitution drafting process. During the period leading to the 2000 Draft Constitution, environmental concerns continued to take a back seat to other issues as the focus of political discourse had shifted to a debate over devolving power. As Sri Lanka already had in place an environmental regulatory regime that extended over two millennia, by 2000 the country's legal framework, along with its progressive judiciary, minimized the need for a constitutional right regarding environmental protection. Interestingly, the landmark decision in Sri Lankan law holding that the right to equal protection included the right to a clean environment occurred only months after Nepal ratified its 2007 Interim Constitution.

Of the factors listed above, only one—judicial receptiveness in Sri Lanka—involved the explicit, verifiable penetration of international norms. Members of the Sri Lankan judiciary have incorporated insights from international soft law instruments such as the Stockholm and Rio Declarations into their decisions in environmental law cases. This progressive form of judicial decision-making has, to a certain extent, convinced environmental groups that they can utilize the existing legal regime to pursue environmental justice without exploring the option of constitutional reform.

Cases and IR questions

Understanding the broader relevance of the comparative study contained in this chapter requires a return to the earlier discussion about environmental rights and central debates within IR. In terms of assessing the role of the state, the cases support the argument stated earlier that the enactment of environmental rights both emphasizes the continued primacy of the state and signals an intrusion into state sovereignty. Members of international civil society acted as agents of norm diffusion by promoting constitutional environmental rights during the drafting of the 2007 Interim Constitution in Nepal, socializing and pressuring relevant decision-makers. In Sri Lanka, environmental rights found their way into the domestic legal infrastructure through the actions of judges, agents of the judicial branch of the state. However, these decisions were assisted by the persuasive use of international environmental law.

Coming back to the question regarding the causal significance of norms, ideational factors implicitly constrained decision-makers while their constitutive effects were less readily identifiable. In Nepal, international norms on human rights, along with the popular demand for environmental protection, constrained decision-makers and shaped the context in which the Interim Constitution was drafted. The emerging international norm of environmental rights had previously been acknowledged and institutionalized by Nepalese justices in the famous *Godavari Marble* case, which was decided in 1995, only three years after "the peak year for constitutionalization of the right to a healthy environment" (Boyd 2012, p.62). Thus, the post-conflict environment in which Nepal sought to develop a new governing charter encouraged harmonization with international norms that were "hard to ignore based on ideological anchorages or political divisions at the domestic level" (Bhandari 2014, p.ix).

In Sri Lanka, norms derived from international environmental law influenced domestic jurisprudence, giving environmental rights the force of legal precedent at the national level. Evidence for the constitutive effects of international norms related to the environment and human rights was less forthcoming. One small example of how norms may constitute the identity of state actors can be seen in the words of Justice Sripavan: "We, the judges of various jurisdictions, as custodians of the rule of law, have a vital role to play in protecting the environment" (Sripavan 2010, p.16). Although not directly referencing human rights, Justice Sripavan recognizes the obligation that judges have to go beyond adjudicating cases and play an active role in safeguarding the environment. As taking such an activist, pro-environmental stance is not a functional requirement of service in the Sri Lankan judiciary, it is possible that given the level of support for environmental protection judges have demonstrated, international norms regarding the environment may help to shape the identity of such actors when they are fulfilling their role as legal experts. Still, the cases do not offer enough empirical evidence to arrive at a more decisive conclusion about the constitutive effects of international norms.

Finally, what do the cases say about the origins of state preferences? The impetus for adopting constitutional environmental rights in Nepal and Sri Lanka appears to have been driven by internal demands to solve environmental problems caused by development and industrialization. Yet, as described in Chapter 1, the origins of environmental rights are located at the global level, not the level of any individual state, and the extent of their pervasiveness varies over time. While the problems experienced by states with constitutional environmental rights may be local, the specific kind of potential solution obtained by environmental rights is itself a product of both history and international society. Therefore, both cases give credence to the observation that state interests evolve over time as the normative environment changes (Florini 1996).

Cases and theory

In addition to addressing major questions in IR, the comparative study also enriches the cognate bodies of literature reviewed in Chapter 2—IR theory, world society theory, and constitutional design theory. In terms of engaging IR theory, Nepal and Sri Lanka illustrate the complex relationship between normative, rationalist–materialist, and domestic politics explanations for the adoption of constitutional environmental rights. Each of these theories offer some explanatory value, and the whole of their combined analytical leverage presents a more complete explanation than any one of the theories standing in isolation.

Norms provided constitution drafters in Nepal with a historically defined constitutional toolkit from which they selected the right to a healthy environment. This kind of provision did not exist prior to 1974, and by 2007 it had become something of a mainstay among the menu of rights states are expected to draw from when writing a constitution. To this extent, norms both constrained the activities of Nepalese constitution drafters by providing a universal constitutional script and, despite the dearth of direct testimony from interviewees alleging as such, constituted Nepal as one country among many that hold environmental rights in the highest regard.

In Sri Lanka, whereas history dictated that the 1978 Constitution would likely not feature environmental rights, the later absence of such rights was a function of politics and limited popular demand, not a lack of effort. Formal adoption of environmental rights had been attempted on at least three occasions, signifying a non-trivial level of desire to see such rights instantiated in the country's legal regime. Far from being unconcerned with environmental rights, Sri Lanka instead stands as an example of a dog that doesn't bark; the cognizable absence of constitutional environmental rights obscures the several failed attempts to adopt them. That they were ultimately integrated into domestic law through jurisprudence points to the persistence of the norm in the face of constant adversity.

In addition, there is reason to suspect that constitutional environmental rights gained special traction in both cases due to their status as a blended norm. As a preeminent norm in international society to which all other regimes and institutions are expected to conform (Shelton 2006, p.293), human rights offer a compelling vehicle for the transmission of secondary norms, such as those related to environmental protection. This creative collision serves a strategic function, since tacking new norms onto existing ones may help to enhance the likelihood that they gain influence (Finnemore & Sikkink 1998, p.908). Constitutional environmental rights allow norms regarding environmental protection to ride the coattails of human rights norms, elevating the importance of safeguarding the environment to new heights that might not be attainable otherwise. The decision to pursue a rights-based approach as opposed to a regulation-based approach is also significant because "rights possess a relatively stronger discursive power" (Morgan 2007, p.15). Thus, in both instances, norms, and more specifically blended norms, played an important role in the decision to enact or attempt to enact constitutional environmental rights.

The cases also demonstrate that the rationalist–materialist explanation was at best half correct. On the one hand, actions or intentions underlying the adoption of constitutional environmental rights in both states clearly exhibited some degree of rationalism. In both instances environmental rights were conceived mainly as innovative policy solutions for environmental degradation. Expectations of the international community aside, constitutional environmental rights were adopted or proposed as rational problem solving techniques. Yet, acknowledgment of this fact does not detract from the possibility that the rational actors who pursued this strategy did so in part because they were enmeshed in the broader normative environment that dictated the range of appropriate actions (Sandholtz 2008, p.103).

On the other hand, similar to the results of the statistical analysis in Chapter 3, the enactment of environmental rights was not found to be related to calculations about maximizing power (e.g., hegemonic coercion) or wealth. If anything, Sri Lanka proves just the opposite; constitutional environmental rights were viewed by some as potential *impediments* to economic growth. In addition, neither case supports the speculation that perhaps states adopt environmental rights to appeal to the siren song of foreign donors or MNCs. Therefore, the successful or attempted instantiation of environmental rights in constitutions in Nepal and Sri Lanka may be a function of rationalist, but not materialist, decision-making.

Finally, the analyses of Nepal and Sri Lanka convey that domestic factors played an important role in explaining the outcomes observed. In the former country, receptivity to international norms depended on environmental conditions, historical contingency, norm entrepreneurship, and political opportunity. In the latter country, the adoption of norms was conditioned by domestic politics, the domestic legal system, and historical contingency. A related cross-national study on the diffusion of legal instantiations of the sustainability principle reached a similar conclusion regarding the impact of domestic processes (Busch & Jörgens 2014). These findings lend support to the arguments that domestic structures (Checkel 1999; Cortell & Davis 2000) and history (North 1990; Sandholtz 2008) matter in the study of institutions and norms. As such, understanding norm expansion requires consideration of the interactive relationship between factors internal to the state and the unique set of conditions present during a specified period of time. Although international norms may inspire changes at the domestic level, the process of transmission is far from "straightforward" (Busch et al. 2012, p.210).

Next, the cases illustrate the utility of approaching the study of norm adoption through the macro-structural lens stipulated in world society theory. While the strict coding criteria and case selection methodology identified Nepal as a country with constitutional environmental rights and Sri Lanka as a country without, the reality buried beneath the veneer of methodological stringency told a different story. As it turned out, both countries had attempted to adopt constitutional environmental rights and had seen environmental rights ensconced in their respective case law. Therefore, the world cultural script comprised of intersecting and mutually reinforcing norms (e.g., constitutionalism, environmentalization, and human rights) was indeed enacted in both states, albeit through a more diverse array of institutional channels than initially anticipated. Such a result confirms a major theoretical expectation held by world society theorists—that world culture will cause institutional convergence in general and structural differentiation in particular settings. In addition, just as world society theory might predict, the historical period in which a constitution was written helped to determine the content contained within. This is because different eras in history dictate "differing modes of institutionalization" (Jepperson 1991, p.151) and promote the adoption of different social norms (Finnemore 1996, p.328).

The comparative study also suggests that ecological modernization insufficiently describes the reasons for the outcomes obtained. As argued in Chapter 2, the advancement of constitutional environmental rights represents both a retreat and reaffirmation of the state, not its disaggregation and partial replacement by the market, as EM theorists allege. On the contrary, the situations in Nepal and Sri Lanka show signs of increased legalization of proposed solutions to environmental problems, a harbinger of amplified state authority. Thus, the analyses conducted here rebuff the EM contention that the rationalization component intrinsic to world culture leads to dramatic state erosion or transformation.

As for constitutional design theory, the cases complicate the view that constitutions are products of either endogenous or exogenous factors. In contradistinction to endogenous scholars, I show that international influences were relevant in the design of both Nepalese and Sri Lankan constitutions. Although the exogenous camp is more forgiving in terms of their willingness to accept that a range of inputs may impact constitutional design, I provide a fuller view of the specific conditions under which certain rights are likely to be enacted in a constitution. As a corollary to this finding, I add the important qualification that just because a right does not appear in the constitution does not mean that it has not been legalized elsewhere. This suggests that theories of constitutional convergence are likely under-inclusive, and studies of this phenomenon should examine the entire legal infrastructure within a country for evidence of isomorphism in order to better capture the empirical reality. The comparative study also identifies and traces specific examples of two forms of transnational constitutionalism—cross-national legal dialogue and constitutional convergence. These examples bolster the claim that these dynamics are part of a global trend. Lastly, I contribute to the small but growing literature on South Asian constitutions in comparative perspective. In particular, I present an uncommon social scientific analysis that touches upon issues of development, governance, human rights, and justice, four concepts that hold "conflicted" implications for constitutionalism within the region (Baxi 2013, p.36).

Finally, how do the analyses of Nepal and Sri Lanka relate to the world cultural framework of constitutional environmental rights expounded in

Chapter 2? First, the cases show that the adoption of environmental rights in both constitutions and case law generally follows the path indicated in Figure 2.1. Elements of world culture (e.g., individualism, rationalization, and universalism) structured the context of the international system, articulating the kinds of norms deemed legitimate to pursue through more concrete means. Intergovernmental organizations (via international law) then translated this macro-structural script into specific international norms. Next, international norms relating to the environment and human rights were advanced by justices in India, the regional norm entrepreneur, transmitted to Nepal and Sri Lanka via constitutional borrowing, and ultimately entrenched in their domestic legal institutions by constitution drafters and judges, respectively. Second, there is reason to suspect, however tentatively, that the incorporation of environmental rights in both instances served to strengthen the burgeoning blended norm at the level of international society, since several countries have enacted constitutional environmental rights since 2007. This cascading norm internalization process and continued propagation suggest that the cyclical orientation of the world cultural framework of constitutional environmental rights may help to describe the dynamics of ideational diffusion in this issue area. In sum, the comparative study illustrates that the world cultural framework of constitutional environmental rights is capable of describing the role that agency and structure play in the diffusion of norms, especially those relating to constitutional environmental rights.

Notes

1 Each country-year that fell below the mean value was coded "0," whereas each country-year with a value above the mean was coded "1."

2 In order to maximize the universe of potential cases for this portion of the study, I defined constitutional events as occurrences involving the passage of a new constitution or the official approval of a draft, interim, or proposed constitution during a given year.

3 While results of the statistical analysis indicated that regional influence was not a significant factor in the adoption of a constitutional right, the fact that both Nepal and Sri Lanka are located in the same region (South Asia) introduced a convenient de facto control for geography.

4 Nepal adopted a constitutional environmental right in its 2007 Interim Constitution, whereas Sri Lanka did not enact such a right either in its 1978 Constitution or 2000 Draft Constitution.

5 For a technical discussion of the research methodology applied in both cases, see the Appendix.

6 Indeed, one interviewee referred to Nepal as a "mosaic" of different ethnic groups (Interview with P. Sharma 2012).

7 One respondent had this to say on the issue of Nepal's economic potential: "We can be rich in 20 years' time if we really manage our water and forest well … We don't have to do anything, we just protect our environment and we protect our local communities, then money will come … We can be rich in a very short time because … there is so much potential" (Interview with B. Pokharel 2012).

8 Logistical and technical support was generously provided by the Southasia Institute of Advanced Studies (SIAS), a well-regarded think tank in Nepal that produces research on development, environmental, and governance issues in South Asia. Information about SIAS can be found on the organization's website, available at www.sias-southasia.org.
9 Although international aid donors possessed "considerable leverage over the policies of Nepal" in the period leading up to the 1990 People's Movement, the donor community ultimately had limited influence during the drafting of the 1990 Constitution (Parajulee 2000, p.224).
10 *Suray Prasad Sharma Dhungel v. Godavari Marble Industries and Others*, WP 35/1992 (1995.10.31).
11 M.C. Mehta has been credited with helping to establish the concept of environmental rights in India through his work as a public interest lawyer (M C Mehta Environmental Foundation 2009). In perhaps his most famous case, Mehta successfully argued that Article 21 of the Indian Constitution, the right to life, should be applied in order to award compensatory damages to individuals harmed by an oleum gas leak. *M.C. Mehta v. Union of India and Ors (Oleum Gas Case 3)*, 1987 AIR 1086, 1987 SCR (1) 819, 1987 SCC (1) 395, JT 1987 (1) 1, 1986 SCALE (2) 1188.
12 *Godavari Marble.*
13 Licht et al. (2007) refer to these elements as constituting the "norms of governance," but I apply the definition to the concept of good governance to accord with Belbase's (2010) construal of the phrase, which is used in the context of discussing environmental good governance in Nepal.
14 Belbase (2009) has advocated in favor of placing a fundamental duty toward the environment in the constitution, although such a constitutional clause would possess even less legal authority than the environmental right articulated in the Interim Constitution.
15 Justice Aryal would later become a powerful advocate of environmental rights during a subsequent constitution drafting process. During a two-day interaction program co-organized by IUCN and Janahit Sanrakshan Manch of Pro Public, a public interest law firm in Nepal, Justice Aryal delivered a presentation to members of the Constituent Assembly entitled, "Clean and Healthy Environmental Rights: Basis for Basic Environmental Rights in New Constitution" (Thapa 2009, p.15).
16 For example, a group of INGOs in Nepal worked together to draft a letter sent to Hon. Laxman Prasad Aryal, head of the ICDC, in which the parties recommended four kinds of provisions related to environmental rights be included in the Interim Constitution. See Care Nepal et al. (2006).
17 For instance, Ms. Sapana Malla, a human rights activist, lawyer, and member of Nepal's Constituent Assembly, and Mr. Narayan Belbase, a well-known environmental lawyer, held meetings with other lawyers and delivered the recommendations of their ad hoc group to other decision-making units within the constitution drafting apparatus (Interview with D. Khanal 2012).
18 The two subcommittees cited most often by interviewees as having a bearing on the ultimate wording of the environmental rights provision were the Fundamental Rights and Directive Principles subcommittee and the Natural Resource and Resource Allocation subcommittee.
19 Political environment, as the phrase is used here, refers to the context *during* the time in which the Interim Constitution was drafted as opposed to contextual factors, discussed earlier, which speak directly to the environment in Nepal *prior* to the constitution drafting process.
20 It was also suggested that the popular awareness of environmental issues was

due, at least in part, to the efforts of civil society organizations (Interviews with D. Khanal 2012 and A. Pokharel 2012).

21 For a discussion of the importance of historical contingencies in fostering changes to legal institutions, see Gellers (2011).

22 A new Sri Lankan Draft Constitution was proposed in 2000 by then President Chandrika Kumaratunga following two drafts composed in 1997, but it met with a controversial defeat in Parliament (Bastians 2013).

23 In-country research support was generously provided by Dr. Camena Guneratne, Professor in the Department of Legal Studies and Dean of the Faculty of Humanities and Social Sciences at Open University of Sri Lanka, and Ira Unamboowe, Executive Director of the American Institute for Sri Lankan Studies' Colombo Center.

24 Fundamental rights featured in the 1978 Constitution include "freedom of thought, conscience and religion, freedom from torture, right to equality, freedom from arbitrary arrest, detention and punishment, rights relating to criminal procedure and the freedoms of speech, expression, assembly, association, culture, occupation and movement" (Wickramaratne 1996, p.27). The absence of economic and social rights in the chapter on "Fundamental Rights" did not mean that such issues were ignored in the 1978 Constitution, however. The chapter on Directive Principles of State Policy and Fundamental Duties, discussed later, did engage economic and social issues, albeit without the explicit use of rights language (Coomaraswamy 1984, p.54).

25 The 1972 Sri Lankan Constitution included a chapter on "Fundamental Rights," many of which were "lifted off the Universal Declaration of Human Rights (UDHR) and the International Covenant on Civil and Political Rights (ICCPR)," and "those rights were to some extent expanded" in the 1978 Constitution (Vinson 2010, p.381). While many of the rights contained in the UDHR appeared in the 1978 Constitution, the right to own property and the right to work were not. In addition, the right to life, liberty and security of person, a provision included in the 1972 Constitution of Sri Lanka, did not appear in the 1978 Constitution (Goonesekere 1988, p.1).

26 One analyst argues that the changes to the enumeration of fundamental rights were overwrought in that "the rights are spelled out too profusely and as a result the restrictions are spelled out equally profusely" (Perera 1979, p.26). For a comprehensive analysis of the differences between the 1972 and 1978 constitutions, see Warnapala (1980).

27 Item three of the Select Committee's questionnaire posed the following question: "What are the other fundamental rights which you would like to be guaranteed in the revised Constitution?" (Jayasuriya 1982, p.64). At the time of writing, I have been unable to obtain the 1978 Report of the Select Committee on the Revision of the Constitution, which describes the results of the questionnaire.

28 The lack of advocacy efforts related to environmental rights may be partly a result of a "rights consciousness" that only began to emerge in the late 1970s (Coomaraswamy 1984, p.48). This issue is addressed in greater depth in the section below on political environment.

29 I did not include among the attempts listed the 2003 National Environmental Policy, which, under Section 4.3 ("Outcomes to be Achieved"), emphasizes that the policy focus on attaining "[a] clean and healthy living environment" and "[a] healthy ambient atmospheric environment," since neither can be considered legally enforceable rights (Sri Lanka Ministry of Environment & Natural Resources 2003, pp.42, 43).

30 Dr. Deepika Udagama, current chairperson of the Human Rights Commission

of Sri Lanka and former member of the subcommittee responsible for drafting the portion of the Bill of Rights concerned with socioeconomic and environmental rights, reports having examined the South African constitution, constitutional jurisprudence of the Indian Supreme Court, and another African constitution in the course of composing the Section 14T's "Right to an Adequate Environment" (D. Udagama, personal communication 2013).

31 Indeed, Justice Kanagasabapathy Sripavan of the Supreme Court of Sri Lanka has acknowledged the importance of the judiciary in safeguarding the environment: "We, the judges of various jurisdictions, as custodians of the rule of law, have a vital role to play in protecting the environment. If we fail to protect the physical factors of the surroundings of human beings, including the land, soil, water, atmosphere, climate, sound, tastes and biological factors of animals and plants of every description, nature would hit us back and if nature really starts becoming furious, we would all be wiped off like ants. Let us hope that man becomes awakened very soon and transforms himself" (Sripavan 2010, p.16).

32 *The Environmental Foundation Limited v. The Attorney-General*, 1(1) S. Asian Envtl. Rep. 17 (S.C. App. No. 128/91, 1992).

33 Founded in 1981, Environmental Foundation Limited (EFL), the "first public-interest law firm in Sri Lanka," was conceived based on the idea that "Sri Lanka possessed a well-developed framework of environmental laws that were ineffectively implemented and which could be used as a lever to promote environmental action" (Guneratne 2008, p.108).

34 *Ashik v. Bandula and Others*, S.C., F.R. App. No. 38/2005, SCM 07.11.2007.

35 However, despite the order from the Supreme Court to enjoin the activities deemed a public nuisance, the "practice continued unchanged" (Pinto-Jayawardena 2010, p.42).

36 *Bulankulama v. Ministry of Industrial Development*, S.C., F.R. App. No. 884/99, 2000.

37 *Watte Gedara Wijebanda v. Conservator General of Forest and Eight Others*, S.C. App. No. 118/2004, SCM 04.05.2007.

38 I deliberately chose to focus on the existence of environmental laws and policies and not their performance since evidence suggests that the implementation of the environmental regulatory scheme in Sri Lanka is seriously inadequate. For instance, in an interview, Lalanath De Silva, a pioneering Sri Lankan environmental lawyer who co-founded Environmental Foundation Limited, states that "[t]wo-thirds of [polluting] industries are operating without a license, illegally, with no controls" (Vinson 2010, p.380). Furthermore, an empirical study of environmental impact statements (EISs) reveals that "despite the existence of a sound legislative framework in Sri Lanka, the analysis contained within EISs generally fails to convey meaningful information to the relevant stakeholders and decision-makers involved in protecting ecological interests and promoting sustainable development" (Samarakoon & Rowan 2008, p.441). Thus, while Sri Lanka has numerous environmental regulations on the books, there appears to be a gap between their enactment and successful implementation.

39 Despite the fact that legal commentators have consistently stated that Sri Lanka does not have a constitutional environmental right *per se*, EFL, the Sri Lankan public interest environmental law firm, has published a handbook that declares unequivocally that "[a] healthy environment is both a right and a responsibility of all Sri Lankans" in the first sentence of a section entitled, "Sri Lankans' constitutional right to a healthy environment" (Environmental Foundation Ltd 2006, p.11). The section mentions the relevant Directive Principles, codes,

ordinances, and acts, but nowhere is an actual constitutional right cited. Thus, it would appear that even in the absence of a fundamental right to the environment instantiated in the constitution, the "most important" (Guneratne 2008, p.105) environmental NGO in Sri Lanka alleges that such a right exists by default.

40 The Sri Lankan judiciary's views on the relationship between Fundamental Rights and Directive Principles of State Policy and Fundamental Duties have shifted over time. Soon after the enactment of the 1978 Constitution, in *Seneviratne v University Grants Commission* [(1978-79-80) 1 Sri L.R. 182] Justice Wanasundera of the Supreme Court, citing Indian Supreme Court precedents, suggested that Directive Principles were equal to Fundamental Rights. Later, in *In re the Thirteenth Amendment to the Constitution Bill* [(1987) 2 Sri L.R. 312)], the Supreme Court "implied that although Directive Principles are not enforceable, Bills may be scrutinised to see whether they represent steps taken in the direction of implementing the programme envisaged by the makers of the Constitution" (Wickramaratne 1996, p.30). However, analysts have also argued that in the event of a conflict between the two, Fundamental Rights reign supreme (Sharvananda 1993, p.107) and "[r]estriction of fundamental rights in the interests of Directive Principles is not permitted" (Wickramaratne 1996, p.32).

41 The right to equality provision states: "All persons are equal before the law and entitled to equal protection of the law" (Sri Lanka Const., art. 12, § 1 (1978)).

42 Specifically, the doctrine of non-arbitrariness has created a "new dimension of equal protection" whereby "anything arbitrary can be challenged" under Article 12(1) (Interview with J. Wickramaratne 2013), suggesting "that the 'gate' that was sought to be shut has in any event been opened in a different way" (Rajepakse 2008, p.141). Unlike the more contemporary issue of protecting human rights in Sri Lanka, the "liberal doctrine of equal protection … became an accepted norm of politics by the early 1950s" (Coomaraswamy, 1984, p.77). Perhaps this fact also helps to explain the propensity of public interest lawyers in the country to bring ostensibly human rights cases under Article 12(1).

43 Yet, as one scholar cautions, "the case law illustrates that the success or failure of public nuisance as a means of environmental protection and the degree of either, is to a large extent dependent on judicial sensitivity, attitude and approach in the particular case" (Puvimanasinghe 1997, p.169). Furthermore, public nuisance prosecutions might not result in the desired environmental outcomes because "there is no procedure for the abatement of nuisance nor direct relief to the victims of such a nuisance" (Puvimanasinghe 1997, p.145).

44 Created in 1980 with the passage of the National Environmental Act, the Central Environmental Authority, the main environmental agency in Sri Lanka, "enforces environmental laws" (Schukoske 1996, p.156).

45 National Environmental Act No. 47 of 1980, Sec. 31.

46 Inspector General's Circular No. 1196/95, Crime Branch Circular No. 05/95, 04.10.1995.

47 EPLs are issued by the CEA and allow "the holder to emit wastes into the environment within stipulated limits and subject to certain conditions" (Environmental Foundation Ltd 2006, p.20).

48 The EIA process is designed "to predict the environmental consequences of development projects and is an important tool to achieve sustainable development" (Samarakoon & Rowan 2008, pp.441–442).

49 One scholar argues that "[EIAs] provide a better source of protection [than nuisance remedies], as they are prospective and can adopt a preventive approach" (Puvimanasinghe 2009, p.45).

50 At the time Sri Lanka's 1978 Constitution was ratified, only two countries in the world had constitutions with environmental rights—Yugoslavia and Portugal. That same year, Spain enacted a constitution with environmental rights over three months later.

Bibliography

Atapattu, S., 1998. A Commentary on the Draft Fundamental Rights Chapter. In Law Society Trust, *Sri Lanka: State of Human Rights 1998*. Colombo: Law & Society Trust, pp.173–191.

Atapattu, S., 2001. Sustainable Development, Myth or Reality?: A Survey of Sustainable Development Under International Law and Sri Lankan Law. *Georgetown International Environmental Law Review*, 14, pp.265–300.

Bastians, D., 2013. Communal Conundrum and Constitutional Calculations. *Colombo Telegraph*. Available at: www.colombotelegraph.com/index.php/communal-conundrum-and-constitutional-calculations/ [Accessed July 3, 2013].

Baxi, U., 2013. Modelling "Optimal" Constitutional Design for Government Structures. In S. Khilnani, V. Raghavan, & A.K. Thiruvengadam, eds. *Comparative Constitutionalism in South Asia*. New Delhi: Oxford University Press, pp.23–44.

Belbase, N., 2009. *Environmental Rights and the New Constitution*, Kathmandu, Nepal: IUCN Nepal. Available at: http://cmsdata.iucn.org/downloads/environmental_rights_in_the_new_constitution.pdf [Accessed March 16, 2013].

Belbase, N., 2010. *Environmental Good Governance in the Future Constitution of Nepal*, Kathmandu, Nepal: IUCN Nepal. Available at: http://cmsdata.iucn.org/downloads/environmental_good_governance_in_the_future_constitution_of_nepal.pdf [Accessed January 23, 2013].

Bhandari, S., 2014. *Self-Determination and Constitution Making in Nepal: Constituent Assembly, Inclusion, and Ethnic Federalism*. Singapore: Springer.

Boyd, D.R., 2012. *The Environmental Rights Revolution: A Global Study of Constitutions, Human Rights, and the Environment*. Vancouver, BC: UBC Press.

Busch, P.-O. & Jörgens, H., 2014. From the Outside in: Explaining Convergence in the Legal Recognition of the Sustainability Principle. In H. Jörgens, A. Lenschow, & D. Liefferink, eds. *Understanding Environmental Policy Convergence: The Power of Words, Rules and Money*. New York: Cambridge University Press, pp.237–264.

Busch, P.-O., Gupta, A. & Falkner, R., 2012. International-Domestic Linkages and Policy Convergence. In F. Biermann & P. Pattberg, eds. *Global Environmental Governance Reconsidered*. Cambridge: MIT Press, pp.199–218.

Care Nepal, IUCN, Winrock International, ICIMOD, The Mountain Institute, & WWF, 2006. Suggestions Given to the Interim Constitution Drafting Committee by INGOs Working in Environment and Biodiversity Conservation, and Sustainable Development. Available at: www.constitutionnet.org/vl/item/suggestions-given-interim-constitution-drafting-committee-ingos-working-environment-and [Accessed December 18, 2013].

Checkel, J., 1999. Norms, Institutions, and National Identity in Contemporary Europe. *International Studies Quarterly*, 43(1), pp.84–114.

Coomaraswamy, R., 1984. *Sri Lanka, the Crisis of the Anglo-American Constitutional Traditions in a Developing Society*. New Delhi: Vikas.

Cortell, A.P. & Davis, J.W., 2000. Understanding the Domestic Impact of International Norms: A Research Agenda. *International Studies Review*, 2(1), pp.65–87.

de Silva, C.R., 1979. The Constitution of the Second Republic of Sri Lanka (1978) and its Significance. *Journal of Commonwealth and Comparative Politics*, 17(2), pp.192–209.

de Silva, K.M., 1981. *A History of Sri Lanka*. Berkeley, CA: University of California Press.

Edrisinha, R., 2007. Conflict and Constitutional Process: Some Sri Lankan Experiences. In H.P. Bhattarai & J. Subedi, eds. *Democratic Constitution Making: Experiences from Nepal, Kenya, South Africa and Sri Lanka*. Kathmandu: Nepal South Asia Center, pp.133–138.

Environmental Foundation Ltd, 2006. *Your Environmental Rights and Responsibilities: A Handbook for Sri Lanka*. Colombo: Environmental Foundation Limited.

Finnemore, M., 1996. Norms, Culture, and World Politics: Insights from Sociology's Institutionalism. *International Organization*, 50(2), pp.325–347.

Finnemore, M. & Sikkink, K., 1998. International Norm Dynamics and Political Change. *International Organization*, 52(4), pp.887–917.

Florini, A., 1996. The Evolution of International Norms. *International Studies Quarterly*, 40(3), pp.363–389.

Gellers, J.C., 2011. Righting Environmental Wrongs: Assessing the Role of Legal Systems in Redressing Environmental Grievances. *Journal of Environmental Law and Litigation*, 26, pp.461–492.

Gilmour, D.A., 1988. Not Seeing the Trees for the Forest: A Reappraisal of the Deforestation Crisis in Two Hill Districts of Nepal. *Mountain Research and Development*, 8(4), pp.343–350.

Goonesekere, R.K.W., 1988. *Fundamental Rights and the Constitution: A Case Book*. Colombo: Law & Society Trust.

Government of Sri Lanka, 1997. *The Government's Proposals for Constitutional Reform*, Available at: www.onetext.org/admin/uploads/The%20Government's%20 Proposals%20for%20Consitutional%20Reform%20Octomber,%201997.pdf [Accessed September 18, 2016].

Guneratne, A., 2008. The Cosmopolitanism of Environmental Activists in Sri Lanka. *Nature and Culture*, 3(1), pp.98–114.

Hachhethu, K., Kumar, S. & Subdi, J., 2008. *Nepal in Transition: A Study on the State of Democracy*. Stockholm: International IDEA. Available at: www.idea.int/publications/nepal_in_transition/index.cfm [Accessed March 21, 2014].

Hill, C.V., 2008. *South Asia: An Environmental History*. Santa Barbara, CA: ABC-CLIO.

Hirschl, R., 2005. The Question of Case Selection in Comparative Constitutional Law. *American Journal of Comparative Law*, 53(1), pp.125–155.

Hutt, M., 1991. Drafting the Nepal Constitution, 1990. *Asian Survey*, 31(11), pp.1020–1039.

ILO, 1989. *Convention (No. 169) Concerning Indigenous and Tribal People in Independent Countries*. Available at: www.ilo.org/dyn/normlex/en/f?p=NORMLEX-PUB:12100:0::NO:12100:P12100_INSTRUMENT_ID:312314:NO [Accessed September 17, 2016].

Inspector General's Circular No. 1196/95, Crime Branch Circular No. 05/95, 04.10.1995.

Jayasuriya, D.C., 1982. *Mechanics of Constitutional Change: The Sri Lankan Style*. Sri Lanka: Asian Pathfinder.

Jepperson, R.L., 1991. Institutions, Institutional Effects, and Institutionalism. In W.W. Powell & P.J. DiMaggio, eds. *The New Institutionalism in Organizational Analysis*. Chicago: University of Chicago Press, pp.143–163.

Karunaratne, W., 2009. *Some Significant Environmental Judgments in Sri Lanka*. Colombo: Environmental Foundation Limited.

Knill, C., 2005. Introduction: Cross-National Policy Convergence: Concepts, Approaches and Explanatory Factors. *Journal of European Public Policy*, 12(5), pp.764–774.

Kumar, D., 2005. Proximate Causes of Conflict in Nepal. *Contributions to Nepalese Studies*, 32(1), pp.51–92.

Licht, A.N., Goldschmidt, C. & Schwartz, S.H., 2007. Culture Rules: The Foundations of the Rule of Law and other Norms of Governance. *Journal of Comparative Economics*, 35, pp.659–688.

M C Mehta Environmental Foundation, 2009. M C Mehta: Environmental Jurisprudence. Available at: http://mcmef.org/environment_jurisprudence.html [Accessed December 24, 2013].

Morgan, B., 2007. The Intersection of Rights and Regulation: New Directions in Sociolegal Scholarship. In B. Morgan, ed. *The Intersection of Rights and Regulation: New Directions in Sociolegal Scholarship*. Aldershot: Ashgate Press, pp.1–22.

National Environmental Act No. 47 of 1980, § 31 (1980).

North, D.C., 1990. *Institutions, Institutional Change and Economic Performance*. Cambridge: Cambridge University Press.

Oli, K.P., 1996. Environmental Compliance and Enforcement: A Case of Nepal. In *Proceedings: 4th International Conference on Environmental Compliance and Enforcement*. Chiang Mai, Thailand, pp.755–776.

Osiatynski, W., 2003. Paradoxes of Constitutional Borrowing. *International Journal of Constitutional Law*, 1(2), pp.244–268.

Parajulee, R.P., 2000. *The Democratic Transition in Nepal*. Lanham: Rowman & Littlefield.

Perera, N.M., 1979. *Critical Analysis of the New Constitution of the Sri Lanka Government, Promulgated on 31-8-78*. Colombo: V.S. Raja.

Pinto-Jayawardena, K., 2010. *Post-War Justice in Sri Lanka: Rule of Law, the Criminal Justice System, and Commissions of Inquiry*. International Commission of Jurists. Available at: http://reliefweb.int/sites/reliefweb.int/files/resources/04234216454178AFC12576B20038FF61-Full_Report.pdf [Accessed April 22, 2014].

Puvimanasinghe, S.F., 1997. An Analysis of the Environmental Dimension of Public Nuisance, with Particular Reference to the Role of the Judiciary in Sri Lanka and India. *Sri Lanka Journal of International Law*, 9, pp.143–171.

Puvimanasinghe, S.F., 2009. Towards a Jurisprudence of Sustainable Development in South Asia: Litigation in the Public Interest. *Sustainable Development Law and Policy*, 10(1), pp.41–49.

Rajepakse, R., 2008. *A Guide to Current Constitutional Issues in Sri Lanka*. Sri Lanka: Citizens' Trust.

Samarakoon, M. & Rowan, J.S., 2008. A Critical Review of Environmental Impact Statements in Sri Lanka with Particular Reference to Ecological Impact Assessment. *Environmental Management*, 41(3), pp.441–460.

Sandholtz, W., 2008. Dynamics of International Norm Change: Rules against Wartime Plunder. *European Journal of International Relations*, 14(1), pp.101–131.

Schukoske, J.E., 1996. Enforcing Environmental Laws in Sri Lanka Through Fundamental Rights Litigation. *International Legal Perspectives*, 8, pp.155–172.

Sharvananda, S., 1993. *Fundamental Rights in Sri Lanka: A Commentary*. Colombo: S. Sharvananda.

Shelton, D., 2006. Normative Hierarchy in International Law. *American Journal of International Law*, 100(2), pp.291–323.

Shrestha, A., 2007. *Necessity of Constitution Assembly in Nepal*. Kathmandu: Kathmandu School of Law.

Sri Lanka Const., art. 12, § 1 (1978).

Sri Lanka Const., art. 27, § 14 (1978).

Sri Lanka Const., art. 28, § f (1978).

Sri Lanka Ministry of Environment & Natural Resources, 2003. *Caring for the Environment 2003–2007: Path to Sustainable Development*. Battaramulla: Ministry of Environment and Natural Resources.

Sri Lanka Ministry of Plantation Industries and Office of Special Envoy on Human Rights, 2011. *Sri Lanka National Action Plan for the Protection and Promotion of Human Rights 2011–2016*. Available at: www.hractionplan.gov.lk/posters/National_action_plan_for_the_protection_and_promotion_of_human_rights_2011_2016_English.pdf [Accessed October 1, 2016].

Sripavan, K., 2010. Judicial Innovations in Environmental Jurisprudence: Sri Lankan Experience. In Asian Judges Symposium on Environmental Decision Making, the Rule of Law, and Environmental Justice. Manila, Philippines. Available at: www.ajne.org/sites/default/files/event/2052/session-materials/kanagasabapathy-sripavan-judicial-innovations-in-environmental-jurisprudence-sri-lankan-exper.pdf [Accessed July 20, 2013].

Thapa, L.B., 2009. *Mainstreaming of Environmental Rights in New Constitution: Right to Clean and Healthy Environment*, IUCN. Available at: www.ccd.org.np/resources/Right%20to%20Clean%20&%20Healthy%20Environment_B%20Thapa.pdf [Accessed December 27, 2013].

Tiwari, B.N., 2007. An Assessment of the Causes of Conflict in Nepal. In Second Annual Himalayan Policy Research Conference. Madison, WI.

UNDP, 2007. *Constitution Making in Nepal: Report of a Conference Organized by the Constitution Advisory Support Unit, UNDP*. Kathmandu, Nepal: United Nations Development Programme.

UNDP, 2015. *Human Development Report 2015: Work for Human Development*, New York: United Nations Development Programme. Available at: http://hdr.undp.org/sites/default/files/2015_human_development_report.pdf [Accessed September 17, 2016].

UN, Sri Lanka, 2015. *Millennium Development Goals Country Report 2014: Sri Lanka*, Colombo: United Nations, Sri Lanka. Available at: www.lk.undp.org/content/srilanka/en/home/library/mdg/sri-lanka-millennium-development-goals-country-report-2014.html [Accessed September 18, 2016].

Upreti, B.R., Ghale, Y. & Ghimire, S., 2010. Food Insecurity and Social Conflict in Nepal. In S.S. Aneel, U.T. Haroon, & A. Salman, eds. *Fostering Sustainable Development in South Asia: Responding to Challenges*. Islamabad: Sustainable Development Policy Institute-Pakistan, pp.141–169.

Vinson, S., 2010. Lalanath de Silva: Sri Lanka Environmental Laws. *Journal of Court Innovation*, 3(1), pp.375–388.

Voigt, C., 2009. *Sustainable Development as a Principle of International Law: Resolving Conflicts Between Climate Measures and WTO Law.* Leiden: Brill.

Warnapala, W.A.W., 1980. Sri Lanka's New Constitution. *Asian Survey*, 20(9), pp.914–930.

Weerasiri, S. & Zhengang, Z., 2012. Attitudes and Awareness Towards Environmental Management and its Impact on Environmental Management Practices (EMPs) of SMEs in Sri Lanka. *Journal of Social and Development Sciences*, 3(1), pp.16–23.

Wickeri, E., 2010. No Justice, No Peace: Conflict, Socio-Economic Rights, and the New Constitution in Nepal. *Drexel Law Review*, 2, pp.427–490.

Wickramaratne, J., 1996. *Fundamental Rights in Sri Lanka.* New Delhi: Navrang.

Wickramaratne, J., Gunatilleke, G., Udagama, D., Nesiah, D., Egalahewa, U., Gamlath, S., Ismail, J., Thalayasingham, F.C., Tamilmaran, V.T., Thangavelu, J., & Yusuf, J., 2009. *Report of the Committee on a New Chapter on Fundamental Rights in the Constitution*, Available at: www.colombotelegraph.com/index.php/full-text-report-of-the-committee-on-a-new-chapter-on-fundamental-rights/ [Accessed September 24, 2016].

Wickremaratne, D., 2004. *Sri Lanka Directory of Environmental NGOs.* Sri Jayawardenapura: Sri Lanka Environmental Journalists Forum.

Wijayadasa, K.H.J., 1994. *Towards Sustainable Growth the Sri Lanka Experience: The Evolution of Environmental Policies and Strategies in Sri Lanka, 1978–1993.* Central Environmental Authority, Ministry of Environment and Parliamentary Affairs.

World Bank, 2015. Nepal Overview. Available at: www.worldbank.org/en/country/nepal/overview [Accessed September 17, 2016].

World Bank, 2016a. Nepal. Available at: www.worldbank.org/en/country/nepal [Accessed September 14, 2016].

World Bank, 2016b. Sri Lanka Overview. Available at: www.worldbank.org/en/country/srilanka/overview [Accessed September 18, 2016].

World Bank, 2016c. World Bank Open Data. Available at: http://data.worldbank.org/ [Accessed September 14, 2016].

Zubair, L., 2001. Challenges for Environmental Impact Assessment in Sri Lanka. *Environmental Impact Assessment Review*, 21(5), pp.469–478.

Chapter 5

Constitutions for a greener future?

Introduction

In this book, I have sought to understand why some countries adopt constitutional environmental rights while others do not. In an effort to answer this question, I embarked on an empirical inquiry in two phases. In the first phase, I conducted a global statistical analysis designed to assess explanations for the emergence of constitutional environmental rights grounded in IR theory, world society theory, and constitutional design theory. In the second phase, I performed a qualitative comparative study that examined how two similar states obtained different outcomes regarding the enactment of constitutional environmental rights. In this final chapter, I seek to accomplish four remaining tasks. First, I summarize the main findings of this project and explain how they relate to the world cultural framework of constitutional environmental rights and major concerns in the field of IR. Second, I provide an update on the status of constitutional environmental rights in Nepal and Sri Lanka. Third, I discuss a range of practical steps states can take to construct a robust environmental rights regime. Finally, I outline directions for future research on this evolving subject at the intersection of human rights and the environment.

Unpacking results of the nested analysis

The interdisciplinary, mixed-methods "nested analysis" (Lieberman 2005) undertaken in this book has yielded new insights regarding the proliferation of constitutional environmental rights throughout the world. Drawing on theory from political science, sociology, and law, I proposed a world cultural framework of constitutional environmental rights that specifies the ideational context from which environmental rights emerged and the causal mechanisms through which environmental rights have percolated from the global (e.g., world cultural) to national (e.g., constitutional) levels. In the first empirical phase of the study, I conducted a global quantitative analysis that examined the extent to which the expansion of constitutional environmental rights could be explained by the process of norm socialization, rationalist–materialist considerations, or domestic politics. Results demonstrated that factors relating to the promotion of international norms (e.g., presence of INGOs in a country) and domestic politics (e.g., history of human rights practices and level of democracy) proved significant, while factors relating to state self-interest (e.g., ability to attract foreign investment and exploit one's natural resources) did not. Seeking to identify explanations not captured by the statistical analysis, the second empirical phase of the study provided a comparative case study of two countries that appeared similar on important dimensions related to the constitutionalization of environmental rights, but obtained divergent constitutional outcomes. The findings reached through this qualitative analysis indicated that, contrary to the expectations laid out in the previous chapter, the likelihood that a state might adopt a constitutional environmental right was mainly affected by factors internal to the state such as the historical context in which a constitution was written and the perceived capacity of existing legal institutions to effectively address environmental challenges.

Given that both the quantitative and qualitative phases of the study emphasized that the enactment of constitutional environmental rights is influenced by a mixture of international and domestic conditions, what more precise conclusions can be drawn and how do they relate to the world cultural framework developed in Chapter 2? First, the results from both phases suggest that while constitution drafting processes may be driven primarily by a desire to attend to domestic concerns, the historical and normative environments in which constitutions are written provide cultural scripts that shape the menu of constitutional possibilities. In this sense, states are to a certain degree constrained by temporal and macro-structural factors during the process of designing a constitution. Second, the extent to which items from this ever-increasing menu are selected depends on a society's level of openness to external ideas, the availability of opportunities to introduce and discuss such ideas with decision-makers, and popular perception regarding the state's ability to manage problems not currently afforded explicit constitutional instruction. The importance of having a national window of opportunity for discussion about the potential legalization of new environmental concepts has been emphasized elsewhere (Pesendorfer 2014, p.233). Third, the content of the constitutional menu is constantly being shaped and reshaped by actors within and beyond the state. Conceptual vagueness, a facet of environmental rights I argued might make their initial adoption more likely, should eventually erode as transnational actors and intergovernmental organizations push to refine the contours of these rights, and states flesh out environmental rights provisions through enabling legislation and the adjudication of environmental rights cases, thus clarifying the nature of state responsibility and the conditions under which litigation might succeed. The world cultural framework of constitutional environmental rights encapsulates the major lessons obtained from this study. It specifies the elements of world culture and international norms that gave rise to environmental rights, indicates the roles played by actors above and below the state in the diffusion of environmental rights, and acknowledges the cyclical dynamic through which environmental rights are continuously redefined by national circumstances and experiences, and become more common globally. In short, the framework accommodates national and international influences, agency and structure, and change and continuity in the context of environmental rights. However, the framework does not function as a predictive tool that enables researchers to forecast where environmental rights are headed next. Such prognostication requires a comprehensive and current mapping of constitutional environmental rights on the books and in practice. To that end, websites such as the Environmental Democracy Index,[1] Environmental Rights Database,[2] and Enviro Rights Map[3] represent important efforts to empirically capture developments related to environmental rights around the world.

As I argued in Chapter 2, the emergence of constitutional environmental rights has received scant attention from scholars of international relations. In an effort to rectify this oversight, I discussed the ways in which studying the emergence of environmental rights might offer new insights regarding important questions in IR. So what lessons related to IR can be drawn from the foregoing nested analysis? First, despite allegations that the state is ill-suited to solve transboundary environmental problems and that transnational actors continue to usurp state authority, "the state remains both a primary site for and an important actor in environmental governance" (Duit 2014, p.3). While the quantitative analysis showed that transnational agents played a role in the adoption of constitutional environmental rights, domestic factors also proved significant. In both Nepal and Sri Lanka, while international or regional actors influenced the design of constitutions and judicial decision-making to a degree, the final determinations laid squarely in the hands of domestic agents. The resolution of environmental challenges animating human rights concerns was not passed along to institutions beyond the state, although the legal technologies invoked to arrive at a solution originated at the level of world culture. In this sense, the emergence of environmental rights has intruded state sovereignty by compelling states to adhere to the postwar constitutional paradigm but it has also allowed the state to retain its pride of place as the primary guarantor of environmental protection for its citizens. Second, results of the study indicate that international norms do affect state behavior. Although direct evidence of the extent to which norms constrained and/or constituted states was not elucidated through the statistical analysis, the case studies provided direct evidence of norms constraining state behavior and indirect evidence of norms shaping the identity of the states themselves. Perhaps most telling was the revelation that despite the apparent absence of explicit environmental rights in its legal infrastructure, Sri Lanka had attempted to enact such rights several times in the past. One could argue that norms did not constrain Sri Lanka's design of a new constitution given the ultimate failure of the effort, but the repeated attempts to formally include environmental rights in the country's legal framework speak to a cognizable persistence, an undeterred knocking at the door of institutional intransigence, to entrench norms domestically. Third, the mixed-methods study contained within these pages suggests that the origins of constitutional choices and state preferences are complex, but in the case of blended norms like environmental rights, some motivations are stronger than others. The survival analysis cast serious doubt on the relevance of material factors like power and wealth in the adoption of constitutional environmental rights while providing evidence that ideational and rational factors internal and external to the state may influence decisions regarding the promulgation of such rights. The comparative study, however, conveyed that while material concerns (specifically the pursuit of economic development) residing in the background may have frustrated the introduction of environmental rights in Sri Lanka, the rational interest in combatting environmental degradation loomed large. Thus, my rejection of the functionalist explanation for enacting environmental rights appears to have been in error. However, while the decisions regarding whether or not to adopt constitutional environmental rights in Nepal and Sri Lanka were mostly instigated by internal conditions, the comparative analysis showed that environmental rights introduced via law and/or jurisprudence owed an intellectual debt to actors and institutions outside national borders.

Nepal and Sri Lanka: an update

The inevitability of change remains a permanent feature among national constitutions. Indeed, the average constitution lasts only about 19 years (Elkins et al. 2009, p.2). Drafting a constitution in the wake of conflict presents a special set of challenges, as countries emerging from conflict are prone to backsliding or transforming into weak democracies (Samuels 2006, p.664). In such post-conflict settings, constitution-making provides an opportunity to draw up a road map to enduring peace. However, the extent to which new constitutions successfully guard against future conflict depends on factors that scholars and practitioners are only beginning to understand (Widner 2008, p.1514). Nepal and Sri Lanka are two countries that have pursued different constitutional paths following the cessation of internal conflict. While Nepal conceived an interim constitution, Sri Lanka has yet to approve a successor to its 1978 Constitution. Yet, since the comparative case study of these two South Asian states was conducted, important constitutional events have transpired. Both countries have experienced changes related to their respective environmental rights regimes.

In Nepal, following deadly protests by minority groups who felt the drafting process "backtracked on addressing structural discrimination" (International Crisis Group 2016, p.i), the 2007 Interim Constitution was replaced by a new constitution on September 20, 2015. Beginning work on a new constitution in 2008, thematic committees within the Constituent Assembly authored separate drafts. Two committees in particular—the Committee on Natural Resources, Economic Rights and Revenue Allocation, and the Committee for Fundamental Rights and Directive Principles—offered contrasting visions regarding environmental rights. The former group left in place the existing environmental rights provision, but added limiting language indicating that the right "shall [not] prevent the enactment of necessary laws for sustainable development" (Constituent Assembly, C. on N.R., Economic Rights and Revenue Allocation 2009, p.16). The latter group took a more progressive tack, expanding the extant environmental right to include "the right to conditioning to safeguard [persons] from the ill effects of climate change" and the right of victims of environmental harm to obtain compensation (Constituent Assembly, C. for F.R. and D.P. 2009, pp.54–55). The final language included in the 2015 Constitution featured elements from both of these proposals, as the solidarity environmental right was joined by a concomitant right to compensation for victims of environmental harm and the stipulation that these provisions should not handcuff the state from passing laws designed to strike "a proper balance between the environment and development" (Nepal Const., pt. 3, art. 30, § 3 (2015)). Thus, while the original environmental right remained intact and a new compensatory right was added, the inclusion of limiting language may be interpreted as an overall weakening of the constitutional environmental right, as the third provision within this article provides a constitutional escape hatch for legislation privileging economic development over environmental protection.

In Sri Lanka, one year after President Maithripala Sirisena took office, Prime Minister Ranil Wickremesinghe initiated the process of crafting a new constitution in January 2016. In an effort to encourage public participation in the design of the constitution, the prime minister established a Public Representations Committee (PRC) on Constitutional Reforms. The PRC's final report suggested that the new constitution include an extensive menu of human rights, including an environmental right: "Every person has the right to a clean and healthy environment, which includes the right to have the environment protected for the benefit of present and future generations through legislative and other measures" (Public Representations Committee on Constitutional Reform 2016, p.103). Significantly, in the text of this provision the PRC included a direct citation to the 2010 Kenyan Constitution. Members of Sri Lankan civil society also expressed their support for the addition of environmental rights. In an open letter to the newspaper the *Sri Lanka Guardian*, nearly 100 organizations and 83 individuals endorsed the PRC's report and called upon the Constituent Assembly charged with drafting the constitution to include, *inter alia*, the right to a "safe, clean and healthy environment" (Thudugala 2016). At the time this book goes to press, it appears likely that a draft constitution will be submitted to the country's Parliament sometime in 2017. Yet, given the fact that environmental rights are not at the top of the public's list of human rights priorities (Center for Policy Alternatives 2016, p.1) and that the U.S. has indicated a desire to assist in the constitution-making process (Jabbar 2016), it remains unclear whether or not environmental rights will find a home in Sri Lanka's new constitution.

New information on the constitutional directions pursued by Nepal and Sri Lanka speaks to the degree to which environmental rights are increasingly considered important elements of contemporary governing charters. However, this observation does not necessarily suggest that their implementation will be unencumbered or their adoption will prove uncontroversial. In any case, these developments warrant close examination, as they stand to contribute additional insights into the practical effects (and limitations) of constitutional environmental rights.

Making environmental rights work

Although the nested analysis performed in this book focused first on theory testing and then theory building, recent efforts to compile anecdotal experiences (UN Human Rights Council 2015) and systematically analyze cross-national data (Gellers & Jeffords 2015; Jeffords 2016; Jeffords & Minkler 2016) have shed new light on the conditions under which environmental rights matter in a practical sense to humans and the environment. Drawing on the lessons learned from these reports, I offer several recommendations for ways to realize the potential of constitutional environmental rights.[4]

First, national constitutions seeking to advance a robust framework for the protection of environmental rights should include the full suite of procedural (e.g., access to information, justice, and participation) and solidarity environmental rights, as well as statements of public policy. Some have argued that procedural environmental rights may be necessary but not sufficient for the realization of human rights related to the environment (Hayward 2004), and the fact that they are so often paired with solidarity environmental rights offers empirical support for this claim (Boyd 2012, pp.66–67). Given the thematic focus shared among the various types of environmental rights, uniting them in a constitution may help to ensure environmental concerns remain front and center throughout the policy process. Therefore, in order to provide the kind of constitutional guidance needed to enact environmental rights, states should instantiate all major forms of such rights in their respective constitutions.

Second, the scope and technical content of constitutional environmental rights should be clarified through enacting legislation. This would allow the public to provide inputs regarding the contours of such rights through their elected representatives, help to institutionalize the goal of protecting environmental rights within governing structures, and assist judges in the adjudication of environmental rights cases by articulating the practical meaning of otherwise ambiguous phrases like a "safe" or "healthy" environment. Accordingly, environmental rights should be woven into all relevant laws and policies (e.g., climate action plans, environmental crimes statutes, and environmental impact assessment laws) in order to increase internal policy coherence and set clear expectations for future legislation pertinent to human rights and the environment.

Third, states should direct resources toward agencies and organizations that promote the implementation of environmental rights. This may involve experimenting with new institutions like green tribunals that offer a specialized venue for dealing with environmental problems and reducing the burden of impacted caseloads in the judicial system. It may also require augmented financial assistance for public interest law firms dedicated to bringing environmental claims on behalf of vulnerable communities. Finally, states may benefit by supporting legal training programs centered on sensitizing judges, lawyers, and policy-makers to environmental law in general and environmental rights issues in particular.

The suggestions offered above represent an indicative, not exhaustive, list of avenues states may pursue if they wish to enhance their capacity to protect environmental rights. While some measures (e.g., adopting procedural environmental rights) should be relatively uncontroversial given that "there is virtually no danger to over-enforcement" (Daly 2012, p.77), other steps (e.g., specifying through legislative means scientifically determined benchmarks of environmental quality that constitute a "healthy" environment) would likely prove more contentious. Ultimately, states will choose the course of action that fits their particular circumstances, converging on the concept of environmental rights while differentiating the manner in which such rights become entrenched into their respective institutions and structures.

Future research

The present work has sought to understand the factors underlying the global trend toward the constitutionalization of environmental rights. The next generation of research on this subject should build upon existing knowledge regarding what environmental rights are, where they can be found, how have they been received by states and regional or international bodies, and why countries do or do not have them, and move toward systematically evaluating their impacts and tracking the evolution of their conceptual interpretation. In the space below I briefly sketch the outline of a research agenda that pushes environmental rights scholarship into new frontiers.

First, researchers should rigorously analyze the effects that environmental rights have on humans and the environment. A few recent works have sought to understand the relationship between environmental rights and environmental outcomes (e.g., Boyd 2012; Jeffords & Minkler 2016), but less is known about how such rights might directly impact humans themselves. Human impacts may manifest themselves in myriad ways. The protection of environmental rights may hold implications for human health, the distribution of environmental goods, or the preservation of cultural heritage among indigenous groups. Outcomes such as these could be explored using a variety of methods, from qualitative focus group interviews to analyses of local-level geospatial data using downscaling techniques (e.g., Jacques 2006). Of course, it is also possible that in the course of protecting the environment using rights-based approaches, human rights may be violated (Conca 2015, p.111). For instance, local community rights might be trampled by environmental advocacy groups seeking to conserve undeveloped land. Simply put, scholars have yet to adequately examine these important potential impacts of environmental rights, leaving much of the empirical landscape relatively undisturbed.

Second, given this study's emphasis on the constraining capacity of international norms, scholars would be wise to follow how changes in the ideational arena shape future constitutions and the meaning of environmental rights. One fruitful area for research involves evaluating how the shifting configuration of power in the international system affects the kinds of rights states decide to adopt. As Law and Versteeg (2011) show, national constitutions appear to be crystallizing around one of two ideological poles—statism and libertarianism. As emerging powers like China and India begin to wield normative clout, hegemonic institutions and models may confront a challenge to their legitimacy (Noesselt 2016, p.654). While the global South has served as "a site of innovation with respect to the human rights-environment interface" (Kotzé 2015, p.189), that reputation may turn depending on the direction that it is pulled in the future. Thus, it may be hasty to assume that environmental rights represent the inevitable conclusion of the global order's interest in both human rights and environmental protection. If the genetic makeup of international society undergoes a recalibration, the world cultural framework of constitutional environmental rights will have to be revised. Another promising area for further analysis centers on the content and application of environmental rights themselves. Set against a backdrop of critical interrogations into law's (in)ability to cope with environmental challenges (e.g.,

Philippopoulos-Mihalopoulos 2011, 2013; Grant et al. 2013; M'Gonigle & Takeda 2013; Woolley 2014), scholars have participated in the creative expansion of environmental rights. For example, Hiskes (2005) argues that environmental rights extend to future generations; Weston and Bollier (2013) would recast the right to a clean and healthy environment as a right to "green governance"; and elsewhere I have suggested that environmental rights should apply in both the natural and built environments (Gellers 2016). Scholarly efforts to broaden or retool the concept of environmental rights may contain seeds that blossom into constitutional innovations. Ecuador's legalization of the rights of nature offers but one example of how environmental rights can evolve over time through the incorporation of ideas that deviate from the established normative order.

This book has sought to forge new ground in the study of constitutional environmental rights by moving beyond normative debates and anecdotal developments in case law (the first wave of research in this area) and comprehensive efforts to describe and categorize such rights around the world (the second wave of research in this area) into the realm of systematic analyses of the expansion of environmental rights using social science methods and theory. However, there is still much that scholars have to learn about the impacts of environmental rights and factors affecting their emergence and interpretation. The projects described above offer only a glimpse of the yet uncharted waters open for exploration.

Conclusion

The challenges facing the planet are well documented. Visual signs of nature's distress dot the physical and digital landscapes. Yet, in a slow, deliberative, and increasingly technological manner, humanity continues to pursue new avenues intended to derail, delay, or simply cope with the realities inherent to the modern world. Constitutional environmental rights represent one of the latest tools humans have conceived to adapt existing institutions to the conditions wrought by industrialization and environmental change in an attempt to achieve resiliency. Thus far, the enforcement of constitutional environmental rights has been infrequent at best and impotent at worst (Christiansen 2013). This does not mean that undertaking a global rights-based approach to environmental protection is a fool's errand, however. As nature cannot "speak" on its own behalf, "environmental questions are, and can only be, *political* questions" (Vogel 2015, p.196). Whether environmental rights can provide a political solution to pressing environmental problems is a question the answer to which the Earth and all its inhabitants are dying to know.

Notes

1 See www.environmentaldemocracyindex.org/.
2 See http://environmentalrightsdatabase.org/.
3 See www.envirorightsmap.org.
4 The recommendations included here draw inspiration from Jeffords and Gellers (2017).

Bibliography

Boyd, D.R., 2012. *The Environmental Rights Revolution: A Global Study of Constitutions, Human Rights, and the Environment.* Vancouver, BC: UBC Press.

Center for Policy Alternatives, 2016. *Opinion Poll on Constitutional Reform.* Colombo, Sri Lanka. Available at: www.cpalanka.org/wp-content/uploads/2016/02/Opinion-Poll-on-Constitutional-Reform.pdf [Accessed September 30, 2016].

Chandraratna, J., 2016. Constitutional Reforms. Lankaweb. Available at: www.lankaweb.com/news/items/2016/09/21/constitutional-reforms/ [Accessed September 30, 2016].

Christiansen, E.C., 2013. Empowerment, Fairness, Integration: South African Answers to the Question of Constitutional Environmental Rights. *Stanford Environmental Law Journal*, 32, pp.215–281.

Conca, K., 2015. *An Unfinished Foundation: The United Nations and Global Environmental Governance.* New York: Oxford University Press.

Constituent Assembly, C. for F.R. and D.P., 2009. *A Report on Thematic Concept Paper and Preliminary Draft 2066 (2009–10 AD)*, Kathmandu, Nepal. Available at: www.constitutionnet.org/files/concept_paper_fundamental_rights_directive_principles.eng_.pdf [Accessed September 29, 2016].

Constituent Assembly, C. on N.R. Economic Rights and Revenue Allocation, 2009. *Report of the Preliminary Draft of the Constitution (with Concept Paper), 2066.* Kathmandu, Nepal: Constituent Assembly Secretariat. Available at: www.constitutionnet.org/sites/default/files/concept_paper_natural_resource.eng__0.pdf [Accessed September 29, 2016].

Daly, E., 2012. Constitutional Protection for Environmental Rights: The Benefits of Environmental Process. *International Journal of Peace Studies*, 17(2), pp.71–80.

Duit, A., 2014. Introduction: The Comparative Study of Environmental Governance. In A. Duit, ed. *State and Environment: The Comparative Study of Environmental Governance.* Cambridge: MIT Press, pp.1–23.

Elkins, Z., Ginsburg, T. & Melton, J., 2009. *The Endurance of National Constitutions.* Cambridge: Cambridge University Press.

Gellers, J.C., 2016. The Great Indoors: Linking Human Rights and the Built Environment. *Journal of Human Rights and the Environment*, 7(2), pp.243–261.

Gellers, J.C. & Jeffords, C., 2015. Procedural Environmental Rights and Environmental Justice: Assessing the Impact of Environmental Constitutionalism. *Social Science Research Network.* Available at: http://ssrn.com/abstract=2646739 [Accessed October 1, 2016].

Grant, E., Kotzé, L.J. & Morrow, K., 2013. Human Rights and the Environment: In Search of a New Relationship. Synergies and Common Themes. *Oñati Socio-Legal Series*, 3(5), pp.953–965.

Hayward, T., 2004. *Constitutional Environmental Rights.* Oxford: Oxford University Press.

Hiskes, R.P., 2005. The Right to a Green Future: Human Rights, Environmentalism, and Intergenerational Justice. *Human Rights Quarterly,* 27(4), pp.1346–1364.

International Crisis Group, 2016. *Nepal's Divisive New Constitution: An Existential Crisis,* Brussels. Available at: https://d2071andvip0wj.cloudfront.net/276-nepal-s-divisive-new-constitution-an-existential-crisis.pdf [Accessed September 29, 2016].

Jabbar, Z., 2016. US to Assist in Drafting New Sri Lankan Constitution. *Sri Lanka Guardian.* Available at: www.slguardian.org/2016/08/us-to-assist-in-drafting-new-sri-lankan-constitution/ [Accessed September 30, 2016].

Jacques, P., 2006. Downscaling Climate Models and Environmental Policy: From Global to Regional Politics. *Journal of Environmental Planning and Management,* 49(2), pp.301–307.

Jeffords, C., 2016. On the Temporal Effects of Static Constitutional Environmental Rights Provisions on Access to Improved Sanitation Facilities and Water Sources. *Journal of Human Rights and the Environment,* 7(1), pp.74–110.

Jeffords, C. & Gellers, J., 2017. Constitutionalizing Environmental Rights: A Practical Guide. Forthcoming in *Journal of Human Rights Practice.*

Jeffords, C. & Minkler, L., 2016. Do Constitutions Matter? The Effects of Constitutional Environmental Rights Provisions on Environmental Outcomes. *Kyklos,* 69(2), pp.294–335.

Kotzé, L.J., 2015. Human Rights, the Environment, and the Global South. In S. Alam, S. Atapattu, C.G. Gonzalez, & J. Razzaque, eds. *International Environmental Law and the Global South.* New York: Cambridge University Press, pp.171–191.

Law, D.S. & Versteeg, M., 2011. The Evolution and Ideology of Global Constitutionalism. *California Law Review,* 99(5), pp.1163–1254.

Lieberman, E.S., 2005. Nested Analysis as a Mixed-Method Strategy for Comparative Research. *American Political Science Review,* 99(3), pp.435–452.

M'Gonigle, M. & Takeda, L., 2013. The Liberal Limits of Environmental Law: A Green Legal Critique. *Pace Environmental Law Review,* 30(3), pp.1005–1115.

Nepal Const., pt. 3, art. 30, § 3 (2015).

Noesselt, N., 2016. Contested Global Order(s): Rising Powers and the Re-Legitimation of Global Constitutionalization. *International Journal of Constitutional Law,* 14(3), pp.639–656.

Pesendorfer, D., 2014. Converging Ideas About Risk Regulation? The Precautionary Principle in National Legal Systems. In H. Jörgens, A. Lenschow, & D. Liefferink, eds. *Understanding Environmental Policy Convergence: The Power of Words, Rules and Money.* New York: Cambridge University Press, pp.209–236.

Philippopoulos-Mihalopoulos, A., 2011. "… The Sound of a Breaking String": Critical Environmental Law and Ontological Vulnerability. *Journal of Human Rights and the Environment,* 2(1), pp.5–22.

Philippopoulos-Mihalopoulos, A., 2013. Actors or Spectators? Vulnerability and Critical Environmental Law. *Oñati Socio-Legal Series,* 3(5), pp.854–876.

Public Representations Committee on Constitutional Reform, 2016. *Report on Public Representations on Constitutional Reform.* Colombo, Sri Lanka.

Samuels, K., 2006. Post-Conflict Peace-Building and Constitution-Making. *Chicago Journal of International Law,* 6(2), pp.663–682.

Thudugala, S., 2016. Sri Lanka: Country & New Constitution. *Sri Lanka Guardian.* Available at: www.slguardian.org/2016/09/sri-lanka-country-new-constitution/ [Accessed September 30, 2016].

UN Human Rights Council, 2015. *Report of the Independent Expert on the Issue of Human Rights Obligations Relating to the Enjoyment of a Safe, Clean, Healthy and Sustainable Environment, John H. Knox: Compilation of Good Practices.* Available at: https://papers.ssrn.com/sol3/papers.cfm?abstract_id=2599011 [Accessed September 30, 2016].

Vogel, S., 2015. *Thinking Like a Mall: Environmental Philosophy After the End of Nature.* Cambridge: MIT Press.

Weston, B.H. & Bollier, D., 2013. Toward a Recalibrated Human Right to a Clean and Healthy Environment: Making the Conceptual Transition. *Journal of Human Rights and the Environment*, 4(2), pp.116–142.

Widner, J., 2008. Constitution Writing in Post-conflict Settings: An Overview. *William and Mary Law Review*, 49(4), pp.1513–1541.

Woolley, O., 2014. *Ecological Governance: Reappraising Law's Role in Protecting Ecosystem Functionality.* Cambridge: Cambridge University Press.

Appendix

Technical discussion of qualitative research methodology

Both case studies were conducted in three phases—(1) interviewee prospecting and interview scheduling, (2) interviewing, and (3) transcribing and analyzing. Each phase is detailed below.

Interviewee prospecting and interview scheduling

Potential interviewees were identified in four ways. First, I contacted individuals suggested to me by colleagues. Second, those individuals provided me with the contact information for other potential respondents whom I then emailed. Third, I supplemented my list of possible interviewees by conducting research to identify people who played an influential role in constitution drafting processes or who possess knowledge of constitutional and/or environmental law in their respective country. Fourth, I established additional interview candidates through the assistance of my colleagues at SIAS in Nepal and Ira Unamboowe, Executive Director of the American Institute for Sri Lankan Studies (AISLS) in Sri Lanka.[1] These processes yielded an initial list of 35 contacts in Nepal and 28 contacts in Sri Lanka.[2] All potential interviewees were then sent an Institutional Review Board (IRB)-approved recruitment letter via email soliciting their participation in the study. In Nepal, once the final list of eight respondents had been established, Kamal Devkota at SIAS assisted me in the scheduling of my interviews.[3] In Sri Lanka, I scheduled interviews through email or phone calls made from my hotel, the Cinnamon Grand Colombo, or at the Colombo Center of AISLS.[4]

Interviewing

During the second phase of the study, I conducted interviews with the eight individuals in Nepal and seven individuals in Sri Lanka. Each interview began with a recitation of the informed consent narrative in order to obtain verbal consent from the interviewee and presentation of a release form that all respondents willingly agreed to sign. All study participants agreed to have their interview recorded on a digital audio recorder. Along with the signed release form and recorded interview, each interview was logged manually on a separate form that included the name of the interviewee, location of the interview, date of the interview, and unique interview code, intended both for record keeping purposes and to provide reassurance that subject identifiable information would remain protected in the event a respondent wished to remain anonymous.

In Nepal, all interviews were conducted at different locations throughout Kathmandu, with the exception of two interviews, which were both held at the main office of the same civil society organization. The interview questionnaire included 32 main questions and 7 subsidiary questions for a total of 39 potential questions.[5] Interviews lasted between 32 minutes and an hour and five minutes long. In Sri Lanka, all interviews were completed at different locations throughout Colombo, with the lone exception being an interview conducted via Skype in my hotel room because the interviewee was in Switzerland at the time.[6] The interview questionnaire included 29 main questions and 5 subsidiary questions for a total of 34 potential questions.[7] Interviews lasted between 15 minutes and 34 seconds and 29 minutes and eight seconds.

Transcribing and analyzing

In the third phase, I began by transcribing each of the interviews in the order in which they were conducted.[8] Each interview was transcribed with the goal of achieving verbatim transcripts, but this was not possible for five reasons: (1) the English language skills of the interviewees ranged considerably; (2) as someone who does not speak Nepali or Sinhala, I found it difficult to discern the precise spelling of certain words spoken by subjects; (3) despite post-interview efforts to obtain clarification on words that were unclear, in many cases where a word was at issue I was unable to decipher it; (4) environmental noise obscured portions of several interviews; and (5) the distance from the speaker to the digital recording device or volume of the respondent's voice occasionally resulted in a reduced sound quality.[9] Despite these issues, all interviews were successfully transcribed with most of the interview data intact. On average it took approximately ten minutes to transcribe one minute of interview data, which translated to over 86 hours of transcribing. Following transcription, emails were sent to all respondents to afford them the opportunity to review the transcript from their interview.

Next, I proceeded to analyze the qualitative data according to steps outlined by Hsieh & Shannon (2005) and Elo & Kyngäs (2008).[10] First, due to the fact that the phenomenon of interest (e.g., the adoption of a specific kind of right in constitutions throughout the world) is not informed by a well-developed body of literature or existing theories, I elected to perform inductive (also called conventional) content analysis on the interview data. This meant that codes and categories would be drawn from the qualitative data itself as opposed to using preconceived codes and categories discussed in relevant literature (Kondracki et al. 2002). Second, I selected the interview as the appropriate unit of analysis (Graneheim & Lundman 2004). Third, I read each interview twice—once in isolation after completing the transcription for a given interview, and all interviews continuously as a single narrative—in order to "achieve immersion and obtain a sense of the whole" (Hsieh & Shannon 2005, p.1279). Fourth, interviews were subjected to open coding, a process by which quotes relating to the phenomenon in question were selected and notes and headings were typed in the margins of the text in order to "describe all aspects of the content" (Elo & Kyngäs 2008, p.109).[11] This initial analysis produced 201 codes from the interviews in Nepal[12] and 25 codes from the interviews in Sri Lanka. Fifth, all highlighted quotes were read over again and resulting codes were categorized into broad groups based on the kind of content conveyed and the ways in which they related to one another. This practice yielded ten broad groups for the Nepal data[13] and two broad groups for the Sri Lanka data.[14] Sixth, I returned to the original research question to engage in the process of abstraction, whereby new categories were generated based on the extent to which they addressed the research topic. This process included using content-characteristic words to define main categories and filing codes into generic categories and subcategories. During this portion of the analysis the original categories were shuffled and condensed, and newly abstracted categories were added. For the Nepal data, the process resulted in the creation of a hierarchical coding structure consisting of 4 main categories, 11 generic categories, and 28 subcategories roughly spanning two periods—before and during the constitution drafting process.[15] For the Sri Lankan data, the process resulted in the creation of a hierarchical coding structure consisting of one main category, four generic categories, five subcategories, and five sub-subcategories pertaining to two important events—the drafting of the 1978 Constitution and the development of the 2000 Draft Constitution. Finally, definitions were composed for every main category, generic category, subcategory, and sub-subcategory, and exemplars for each were drawn from interview data. These resources became the official code books for the study.

Notes

1 The American Institute for Sri Lankan Studies is a non-profit organization and professional association established in 1996 to "promote US research and teaching on Sri Lanka and to build mutually beneficial links between US and Sri Lankan scholars and institutions." For information about AISLS, please visit the institute's website, available at www.aisls.org/.

2 While in Colombo, I established nine new contacts and visited Environmental

Foundation Limited (http://efl.lk/), an environmental public interest law firm, and the Institute of Human Rights (http://ihrsrilanka.org/), a civil society organization dedicated to the protection of human rights in Sri Lanka.

3 During my time in Nepal, I had as many as three interviews scheduled on a single day and only two days in which no interviews were scheduled.

4 During my time in Sri Lanka, I had a maximum of two interviews scheduled on a single day (twice) and three days on which no interviews were scheduled, mainly as a result of cultural or religious holidays (Madin Full Moon Poya Day on March 26 and Good Friday on March 29).

5 During the course of the interviews, it became clear that the number of questions asked of the respondents would need to be reduced significantly in order to utilize the interview time effectively. Therefore, interview time was mainly focused on obtaining responses for ten of the most important questions from the original questionnaire. In addition, the semi-structured design of the interviews made it essential to stick to a limited set of questions in order to leave time for ad hoc follow-up questions.

6 Interview sites included the Central Environmental Authority, Citizens' Trust, International Centre for Ethnic Studies, and World Bank, as well as private residences.

7 Due to the variations in personal and professional experiences of the interviewees and time constraints, the number of questions posed during interviews was significantly less than the total number of questions originally devised for the study. A quantitative analysis of the interview transcripts indicates that, on average, I asked each respondent approximately 11 questions, some of which did not appear on my questionnaire but were relevant to each interviewee, their line of work, and the responses they provided to certain questions.

8 Interviews were transcribed using f4, a transcription software tool.

9 Where the identification of a particular word remained unclear, I indicated as such on the transcript by placing the word in question in brackets alongside a question mark (i.e. [constitutionalism?]).

10 I chose to employ qualitative content analysis as opposed to quantitative content analysis due to the relatively low number of interviews conducted. Therefore, throughout the analysis, no attempt was made to quantify the frequency with which certain codes appeared in the interviews, as such an effort would have run afoul of the threshold needed to make viable statistical inferences.

11 Interviews were analyzed using ATLAS.ti 7, a qualitative analysis software tool.

12 Two important caveats about the coding process for this project are relevant here. First, I deliberately did not code information regarding the development of Nepal's failed 2012 constitution or issues not directly germane to the drafting of the 2007 Interim Constitution and/or environmental rights, such as one interviewee's lengthy discussion of ethnic cleavages and demographics. Second, I did not amend statements made by interviewees or attempt to harmonize codes by making inferences that I could not substantiate. For example, one respondent referred to a group of civil society actors as the "Natural Resource People's Parliament," whereas another respondent spoke of a "Natural Resource Network." While it is likely that both interviewees were referring to the same group, I coded them differently. The result of this cautious approach to coding is that the original number of codes was likely inflated due to redundancies. However, this problem was ameliorated as codes were filed into generic categories and subcategories and the analysis focused more on contextual factors and political dynamics rather than the number of groups that participated in the constitution drafting process.

13 The ten categories were case, country, event, group, institution, international law, key actor, political debate, process, and rationale.
14 The two categories were law and rationale.
15 While a sincere effort was undertaken to code for all potentially relevant ideas and concepts, only those codes that were determined to be directly related to the task of explaining the adoption of the constitutional environmental right in the Interim Constitution are discussed here. Mainly, codes pertaining to the mechanics of the drafting process itself are omitted, and the array of relevant actors is discussed when necessary. Effectively, this means that this Appendix only describes 2 main categories, 6 generic categories, and 20 subcategories derived from the coding process.

References

Elo, S. & Kyngäs, H., 2008. The Qualitative Content Analysis Process. *Journal of Advanced Nursing*, 62(1), pp.107–115.

Graneheim, U.H. & Lundman, B., 2004. Qualitative Content Analysis in Nursing Research: Concepts, Procedures and Measures to Achieve Trustworthiness. *Nurse Education Today*, 24(2), pp.105–112.

Hsieh, H.-F. & Shannon, S.E., 2005. Three Approaches to Qualitative Content Analysis. *Qualitative Health Research*, 15(9), pp.1277–1288.

Kondracki, N.L., Wellman, N.S. & Amundson, D.R., 2002. Content Analysis: Review of Methods and their Applications in Nutrition Education. *Journal of Nutrition Education and Behavior*, 34(4), pp.224–230.

Index